Tatemae and Honne

Tatemae and Honne

Distinguishing Between
Good Form and
Real Intention in
Japanese Business Culture

Mitsubishi Corporation

THE FREE PRESS
A Division of Macmillan, Inc.
NEW YORK

The Free Press
A Division of Macmillan, Inc.
866 Third Avenue, New York, N.Y. 10022

Collier Macmillan Canada, Inc.

Printed in the United States of America

printing number

1 2 3 4 5 6 7 8 9 10

Library of Congress Cataloging-in-Publication Data

Tatemae and honne: distinguishing between good form and real intention in Japanese business culture/Mitsubishi Corporation.
    p.   cm.
   ISBN 0–02–921591–9
    1. Japan—Commerce—Terminology. 2.Japan—Civilization—
Terminology. I. Mitsubishi Shōji Kabushiki Kaisha.
HF1002.5.T38   1988
302.3′5—dc 19

                                                         87-33226
                                                             CIP

Foreword

The Greek *logos*, meaning word, is also used to signify cosmic reason, essence, rule, etc. The thoughts and actions of a people were expressed in words, and, it could be said, words in their turn molded patterns of thinking and behavior. Truly, words constitute culture and reflect a people's history, manners, and customs.

For the past eight years or so, the English-language *Tokyo Newsletter*, published every month by Mitsubishi Corporation, has been attempting to explain some typical Japanese expressions in its "Business Glossary" column. The column introduced unique Japanese business practices and expressions in a light but informative form. In order to compile this volume, more than forty items were added to those first published in *Tokyo Newsletter*.

In selecting the expressions, old Japanese proverbs and ancient Chinese expressions (such as **bokushu,** meaning inflexibility or running against the current of the times to stick to old ways) have been avoided. Also left out were frequently used business expressions that could be rendered simply in English as one word (such as **ōte,** meaning checkmate). The expressions selected were those which figure in the daily conversation of Japanese businessmen, who understand them instantly, but which might create misunderstanding among people of other countries unless some supplementary explanation is given. Therefore, the selections are in no way intended to constitute a comprehensive glossary.

At the same time, it means that almost all of the expressions need no explanations for the Japanese reader. Moreover, the bulk of the explanations were written originally in English (by Kazuma Uyeno of Century Eibun Henshusha, Ltd.) and were translated into Japanese for the purposes of this volume. Because things which are absolutely unnecessary as explanation for Japanese have been left out, the reader is forewarned that the translation is not necessarily faithful to the original. However, some of the newly added items were first written in Japanese and translated into English as faithfully as possible.

This was first published as *Japanese Business Glossary* by Toyo-Keizai-Shinposha.

The editor would feel amply rewarded if this small volume should provide topics for conversation between Japanese readers and their foreign friends and help smooth the way for better international communication.

JUNICHI NAKAMURA
General Manager
Corporate Communications Office

Simplified Pronunciation Guide

In order to pronounce correctly the Japanese words listed in this glossary, all you need do is learn the pronunciation of five vowels. The Japanese syllabary, which corresponds to the English alphabet, represents far fewer sounds than the letters of the alphabet. The syllabary contains only five vowels, thirteen "semiconsonants" and one consonant—in all, seven less than the letters in the English language. (For the purposes of this simplified guide, we call the syllabary symbols that start with a consonant sound but end with a vowel sound "semiconsonants.")

The table on the next page renders the Japanese syllabary in alphabetical letters. It also gives the diphthongs. The vowels and consonants are always pronounced in the same way, without exception.

The constant pronunciations of the vowels are:

"a" as in announce   "e" as in pen
"i" as in ink   "o" as in oil
"u" as in put

The vowels which appear in the syllabary as part of the semiconsonants are always pronounced as shown above.

There are cases in which the vowel sound is prolonged. In such cases, in this book they are indicated with a macron above the vowel: ā, î, ū, ē, ō.

A guide for pronouncing the consonant sounds is not necessary, because when, say, "k" is coupled with the constant sound of any of the five vowels, it can have only one possible sound. The only consonant that needs an explanation is "g." This is always hard, as in the English word **go**.

The diphthongs are combinations of some of the semiconsonants with the "y" line semiconsonants ending in "a" or "u" or "o." In this case, the vowel sound of the prefixed semiconsonant is eliminated.

With one exception, all Japanese words expressed in the English alphabet end with a vowel. The exception is "n." This is pronounced in a nasal way in much the same way as the English "-ng," but without sounding the "g." The consonant comes only at the end of a syllable, and therefore in the words in this glossary, it is always followed by a semiconsonant: **banzai, hanko, denshin,** etc.

Sometimes, you will find double consonants in the middle of a word, such as **chotto** and **ippai.** In this case, the preceding vowel is pronounced with a slightly rising inflection and the first of the double consonants is choked.

When two vowels come together, pronounce

each separately; do not run them together: **shain** = sha·in; **teate** = te·ate.

Japanese Syllabary Expressed in Alphabetical Letters

Vowels	a	i	u	e	o

Semiconsonants

	a	i	u	e	o
"k" line	ka	ki	ku	ke	ko
"s" line	sa	shi	su	se	so
"t" line	at	chi	tsu	te	to
"n" line	na	ni	nu	ne	no
"h" line	ha	hi	fu	he	ho
"m" line	ma	mi	mu	me	mo
"y" line	ya	i	yu	e	yo
"r" line	ra	ri	ru	re	ro
"w" line	wa	i	u	e	wo
"g" line	ga	gi	gu	ge	go
"z" line	za	ji	zu	ze	zo
"d" line	da	ji	zu	de	do
"b" line	ba	bi	bu	be	bo
"p" line	pa	pi	pu	pe	po

Consonant

The one consonant is "n," which comes only at the end of a syllable.

Diphthongs

kya	—	kyu	—	kyo
sha	—	shu	—	sho
cha	—	chu	—	cho
nya	—	nyu	—	nyo

hya	—	hyu	—	hyo
mya	—	myu	—	myo
rya	—	ryu	—	ryo
gya	—	gyu	—	gyo
ja	—	ju	—	jo
bya	—	byu	—	byo
pya	—	pyu	—	pyo

Abura wo uru

"What is he doing?" "He's selling oil." This is a respectable activity, but if the answer were translated directly into simple Japanese, it can take on a derogatory meaning describing the way a person applies himself to his job. This is because **abura wo uru** has another meaning besides "to sell oil." The other meaning is "to loaf on the job."

In the days before electricity, street vendors went around town selling rapeseed oil for use in lanterns. As they seemed never to be applying themselves very assiduously to their work, the term **abura wo uru** was born; nowadays it is frequently used to describe a businessman who slips out of the office to pass the time in a coffee shop.

Ago

In some cases where an English metaphoric expression uses the word "nose," the Japanese counterpart uses the word **ago** (chin). According to one wag, this is because the Japanese have flat noses, which are not very expressive, and it is easier for them to move their chins. Anyway, **ago de tsukau** (use with the chin) means "lead by the nose" and **ago de ashirau** (handle with the chin) means "turn up one's nose" at someone.

A dictatorial boss disregards the feelings of his subordinates and "drives them with the chin"; if the subordinate should voice dissatisfaction, the boss would thereafter "handle him with the chin."

Even a competent and humanistic boss would sometimes set a high target for a subordinate to attain and order him to attain it. When the subordinate does his very best but is unable to attain the target, he would **ago wo dasu** (stick out his chin), which means "get exhausted."

It can be said that the boss who manages his people with this in mind is an outstanding boss. He will know how to listen to his subordinates' woes and comfort them while drinking with them at an **aka-chōchin**.

See also Aka-chōchin.

Aisatsu-mawari

After the weeklong year-end and New Year holidays, government offices and commercial houses reopen for business on January 4 or 5. But the foreign businessman who visits a Japanese company on that day expecting to conduct business is often frustrated.

Offices reopen, but the main business of the day, after the employees have listened to the president's traditional New Year speech in which he outlines his plans and expectations for the new year and exhorts the staff to greater endeavors, is **aisatsu-mawari**. **Aisatsu-mawari** is "making a round of courtesy calls." The employees make calls not only on people in other departments of the same company but also on outside clients to say, "Happy New Year! Please continue to favor us again this year."

The term is not limited to New Year's courtesy calls. The courtesy calls an executive makes when he takes up a new post in Japan are also **aisatsu-mawari.**

See also Gashi-kōkan.

Aka-chōchin

Many Japanese corporate workers make it a habit to drop in at an **aka-chōchin** before they head for home after a day's work. **Aka** means red and **chōchin** lantern, but don't jump to the conclusion that the phrase means a ''red light'' establishment.

This huge lantern, about a meter in diameter and made of paper pasted over bamboo ribbing, is prominently displayed in front of typical Japanese drinking establishments. It is an indication that the shop serves **sake** and simple popular dishes, that its prices are cheap, and that an informal camaraderie prevails. A person can enjoy himself for a couple of hours at a cost of less than ten dollars. The **aka-chōchin** may be considered the Japanese counterpart of the English pub.

In addition to the red lantern, there hangs above the doorway a **nawa-noren,** a short curtain with the shop's name on it. Thus, both **aka-chōchin** and **nawa-noren** can be used to mean an inexpensive drinking place.

See also Noren, Chotto ippai.

Aku

This is the Japanese word for ''lye,'' which is made by mixing ash with water. The Japanese word also refers to the strong astringent fluid found in some plants. From this, the word began to be used in describing a person of somewhat unrefined personality who is very self-assertive.

Kare wa aku ga tsuyoi (he is strong in lye) means that the person is strongly self-assertive, high-handed, and abrasive. Such a man, of course, is not popular among his fellows. Sometimes an aggressively able person is so described by jealous colleagues.

On the other hand, **kare wa aku no nuketa hito da** (he is a man with the lye extracted) means a refined or polished person who has no offensive traits, who is not greedy and not affected. He is the type who is liked by all around him. However, this expression is often used sarcastically in reference to a person who lacks spirit. Therefore, if you are so described it may be the better part of wisdom not to become instantly elated but to ponder the nuance.

Ama-kudari

Ama-kudari is written with the Chinese ideograms that mean ''to descend from heaven.'' The character for **ama** (heaven) stands for the emperor, shogun, or the central government. The expression is used to mean the taking of a top post in a private company by a person who has retired from high government office.

Ama-kudari is also used to refer to a person coming from a different division in a government ministry or business corporation to become the head of another division or section, or to a manager in a parent company being appointed president of a subsidiary.

In Japan, personnel shifts between companies are rare, and the manager of a department in a big corporation is almost invariably promoted from among the staff of that department. Consequently, an **ama-kudari** appointment has a somewhat unpleasant meaning to the staff of a department receiving a manager from the outside.

In Japan of the Middle Ages, the word **ame no shita** (literally, under the heaven) meant not just all Japan but the entire world. Another way of pronouncing the ideogram for **ame no shita** is **tenka,** and even today election as the prime minister of Japan or an exceptional rise to a top position is referred to as **tenka wo toru** (to take or seize power).

See also Teiki-saiyō, Sekigahara, Tozama.

Aota-gai

Aota-gai is a phrase that originally was used in agriculture. Today it is scarcely used in farming communities but has become an indispensable part of the industrial vocabulary.

In the old days it meant "buying rice on the stalk," before it is harvested. It is similar to buying beef on the hoof or wool on the sheep's back. Poor farmers in need of cash received money from merchants in exchange for a promise to deliver the rice when harvested.

Aota-gai (literally, to buy a green paddy field) is used today to describe the act of companies "raiding" schools to "sign up" students scheduled to graduate in the spring of the following year. Sometimes, instead of **aota-gai,** people use **aota-gari** (to harvest the green paddy) to describe the intensity with which companies conduct their premature recruiting.

See also Shin•nyū-shain.

Apointo

The Japanese lexicon is full of words borrowed from foreign languages, altered somewhat in form and sometimes even in meaning to make them fit into Japanese life. **Apointo** is a corruption of "appointment."

Although it is used in the standard sense to mean a prearranged meeting, it is not uncommon for a visitor with an **apointo** to be kept waiting because someone got there before him, quite often a person who dropped in without an appointment. The fact that a person "just happened to be in the neighborhood" is sufficient reason to gain entry, because a Japanese executive or a knowledgeable foreign businessman in Japan rarely refuses to see someone who drops in without an **apointo.**

In all fairness, however, it must be said that the younger breed of international-minded Japanese businessman is more scrupulous about strictly keeping appointments.

Arubaito

Arubaito is not a native Japanese word but the Japanized form of the German word "arbeit," meaning "work." As in the case of thousands of foreign words the Japanese have adopted, the original meaning has been changed to suit Japanese purposes.

Thus **arubaito** refers to part-time work, temporary work, or moonlighting. Students who work to earn pocket money or to pay tuition are doing **arubaito.**

Companies often carry a category of workers called **arubaito** who work regular full hours but are treated differently from regular employees. They are paid by the hour or by the day and are not given any of the substantial fringe benefits of regular employees. Piecework **arubaito** is usually done at home.

See also Naishoku.

Asameshi-mae

The child who stays up late watching TV and gets up too late in the morning to eat breakfast before rushing off to school; the dieting young woman who skips breakfast—both start their day's activities **asameshi-mae** (before breakfast) or, in other words, before having a bite to eat. When a person's stomach is empty, he naturally lacks the energy to do substantial work.

Thus, when one says, "That's **asameshi-mae**," he means "For me that job is easy as pie. I could even do it on an empty stomach." A similar expression is **ocha-no-ko sai-sai,** which means work that can be done even on a lightly filled stomach (**ocha-no-ko** = tea cakes or light refreshment).

Both expressions are usually in the first person to boast of one's own ability or competence. However, when others use them in a way which is flattering to you, watch out. When you are already up to your neck in work, your boss may call you and say, "This is aside from what you are doing now, but please get it done by such-and-such date. You appear to be busy, but this is **asameshi-mae** for you, isn't it?" If you should swallow his flattery, your work load will be doubled.

See also Ocha (wo nigosu), Ōwarawa.

Ate-uma

This word originally meant a stallion brought near a mare to excite and make her ready for the stud horse. The stallion is never the main actor. **Ate** = apply; **uma** = horse. Nowadays, the word is also used to refer to any device—a tool, a draft plan, a candidate, etc.—employed to find out what the other party is really thinking or intending.

Although Company X intends all along to give the construction contract to Company A, it holds a public tender and invites companies B and C to compete. The contract goes to Company A anyway. In such a case, companies B and C are said to have used as **ate-uma**.

Among other expressions containing the word **uma** are **tsuke-uma** (attached horse) and **yaji-uma** (**yaji** = cheer, root, hiss, boo).

In the old days, when a person who had enjoyed a night on the town did not have enough money to pay the bill, he went home with a money collector trailing behind him. This money collector was called **tsuke-uma**. Nowadays shops don't use **tsuke-uma**. They call the police.

Yaji-uma is a person who is so full of curiosity that he abandons whatever he is doing, even work, to rush to the scene of a fire, an accident, or a fight.

Ato-no-matsuri

Ato is "after" and **matsuri** is "festival," but **ato-no-matsuri** is not the name of a particular kind of festival. The term is used to describe either festival equipment that has arrived too late for use in the festival or people who have come too late to see the festival. Thus, it is used to mean "too late to be of any use, too late for treatment, past cure" or "out of date."

The original meaning was "post-death festival" or a funeral. Its origin suggests the thought that no matter how splendid the festival, if it is held after one's death, it gives no pleasure, because the dead cannot experience it.

Today, the word is used in the meaning explained in the first paragraph. Other "too late" expressions are **kenka sugiteno bōchigiri** which means "It's no use bringing a stick after the fight is over" and **muika-no ayame, tōka-no kiku** which means that it is too late to go to see the iris (**ayame**) on May 6 (**muika**) or the chrysanthemum (**kiku**) on September 10 (**tōka**) because it would be one day after their respective festivals are over.

And yet, the Japanese appreciate a moon past its full phase—on the sixteenth and seventeenth nights—as much as the full moon, which comes on the fifteenth night of the lunar calendar.

Banzai

Do not be frightened when you hear a group of Japanese shouting **banzai** in an airport lobby. It is not the **banzai** attack cry heard in World War II movies; rather, they are sending off one of their colleagues leaving for an overseas post.

Banzai is literally "ten thousand years." On the Emperor's birthday, thousands of people gather in the courtyard of the Imperial Palace to chant **banzai,** in which case it means "Long live the Emperor."

Banzai is also a simple "hurray" for felicitous occasions. Winning a baseball game, completing a building, getting elected to office, or finding the right word for a crossword puzzle calls for a **banzai.** Surrounded by friends and relatives at a railway station, newlyweds are sent off on their honeymoon with a rather embarrassing, attention-attracting **banzai.**

Batsu

Batsu is an important institution in Japanese society. Knowing what **batsu** a certain person belongs to helps greatly in constructing your human relations in the society. In general terms, **batsu** means clique, faction, or clan.

There are various types of **batsu.** Major Japanese

political parties often have factions (**ha-batsu**), which are like parties within the party. Each faction is constituted around an influential politician and is usually known by his name.

The **kei-batsu** is not necessarily an organized group as such, but it speaks with a loud voice. It can be the clan whose members are linked together by blood and marriage. People in the process of climbing into the higher rungs of society through business success, political power, or other means make every effort to get their sons and daughters married into high society, an arrangement that will be advantageous to them.

The **gaku-batsu** is the alma mater clique. If a young man joins a company where men from his university are dominant, **gaku-batsu** sectarianism will favor him in promotions. On the other hand, if a person belongs to a minor **gaku-batsu** in the company, he has no chance of rising to a high executive position no matter how able he may be. In recent years, the **gaku-batsu** element has become less important in the business world, although it is still strongly entrenched in the bureaucracy and in academic circles.

Another one is **chihō-batsu.** This can be regarded as a form of sectionalism, because **chihō** means ''district'' or ''region.'' Persons who come from the same region of the country are regarded as belonging to that area's **batsu,** and they tend to help and favor each other. However, thanks to the high demographic mobility of recent years, people are beginning to place less emphasis on this **batsu.**

Benkyō

Benkyō is "study," and **benkyō-suru** is "to study." Thus one can easily understand when it is used in the meaning of "diligent, industrious."

But when the housewife goes to the corner grocery, picks up a head of lettuce, and says to the shopkeeper, "Won't you **benkyō** this a bit more?" she certainly couldn't be telling him to study the lettuce. And when the shopkeeper replies, "Since you're a regular customer, I'll **benkyō** 50 yen," he couldn't mean he'll study the 50-yen coin. In this case, the word means "discount."

Giving a discount was associated with the willingness of the merchants to work hard to realize a fast turnover, because they believed in increasing total profit by selling in volume at a small margin.

With the rise of supermarkets, where goods are sold at listed price—and no bargaining, please—housewives have lost a place where they can say **Benkyō shinasai** (give me a discount). Is it preposterous to say that perhaps it is in reaction to this that they have become so insistent these days in telling their children **Benkyō shinasai** (study hard)?

See also Sābisu.

Bōnasu

Japanese salaried workers receive extra wages in the form of a bonus, pronounced **bōnasu** by Japanese, twice a year, normally in June–July and December. The amount averages between one and three months' equivalent of the monthly salary.

The bonus was originally a profit-sharing system. Before World War II, the management of a company that enjoyed good business during the preceding half-year period paid a large bonus (sometimes the equivalent of six months' salary or more). In bad times there was little or no bonus.

Today, workers regard the bonus as an integral part of their annual salary. They cover their day-to-day expenses with their monthly pay and use the bonus for buying expensive clothes and durable goods. A good part of the bonus is salted away for future expenses, such as the children's education. This is one of the reasons why the Japanese savings rate is so high. Labor unions claim the bonus is a form of deferred payment of compensation to which the employee is entitled. Strikes over the amount of the bonus are not unusual.

Bōnen-kai and Shin·nen-kai

For Japanese businessmen, December is the month of the **bōnen-kai** office party. As the characters in the ideogram (forget-year-party) show, it is a function to wind up the year. Each section of a large company holds its own **bōnen-kai,** with every member chipping in to cover the cost. Because the year-end party is universal, tables in restaurants have to be reserved well in advance.

Alcohol flows freely—how else can the memories of the year's failures, frustrations, disappointments, and irritations be washed down the river of time? Of course, the better, happier occasions are remembered with appropriate toasts.

With the past thus buried, or pickled in alcohol, everyone is ready to make a fresh start with the coming of the New Year. Some groups also hold a New Year party (**shin•nen-kai**), but usually they have only one or the other.

See also Bureikō.

Buchō

The **buchō** is the chief of a division, reporting to the managing director or the president of a company. Some **buchō** are members of the board of directors.

The traditional Japanese job description of the **buchō** is that he participates in interdivision meetings and chairs the intradivision meetings. The role of the **buchō** in the big companies is similar to that of the president of a member enterprise of a large American conglomerate, but the *modus operandi* is somewhat different.

For example, the **buchō** seldom dictates letters to his secretary. In fact, not many **buchō** have one. Instead, he tells one of his subordinates what kind of a letter needs to be sent out. The draft is written at a lower level and comes up for the **buchō**'s signature by way of the **kakarichō** (subsection chief) and the **kachō** (section chief).

See also Kachō.

Bureikō

Bureikō originally meant a meeting of people who were on intimate terms, regardless of rank. Nowadays, we hear this word at a New Year's party (shin•nen-kai), year-end party (bōnen-kai), and company excursion (shain-ryokō) in the form, "Let's go **bureikō** today." This means "Let's leave aside rank and seniority today and have a good time drinking." In other words, it indicates that a lack of formality will be tolerated.

But even though there will be no standing on ceremony, people with organizational titles will still be addressed as "**Buchō**" or "**Jōmu**" instead of "**-san.**"

See also Bōnen-kai, Shain-ryokō, -San.

Cha-bōzu

Cha is tea and **bōzu** is a Buddhist priest. This was the name given in the old days to the lowly samurai whose duty was to serve tea in the shogun's castle. Like a priest, his head was shaved and he wore the priest's raiments, signifying a person who wants to live in a world that transcends status and class. In order for a lowly samurai, whose work was the lowly one of serving of tea, to serve the shogun, it was probably necessary for him to transcend status.

Even though the **cha-bōzu**'s task was menial, the fact that he served so close to the shogun often made him act haughty toward others in reflected glory. Thus the word began to take on a scornful meaning as a way of referring to people who curry favor with persons in authority or who get the notion that they are the favorite of the man in power and act high and mighty toward others.

One finds **cha-bōzu** in every society. The **cha-**

bōzu may really think that he is acting as a loyal company man. And those who criticize him as "that damned **cha-bōzu**" may be feeling self-pity because they aren't as clever in currying favor with their boss.

See also Gomasuri, Ocha.

Charan-poran

"He is **charan-poran**" is a disparaging remark meaning that the person is unreliable in what he says and that he gets out of a tight situation by telling the first lie that comes to his mind. A **charan-poran** person does not have staying power and will abandon a task midway and go off aimlessly on a tangent. Although the word does not suggest that such a person is evil by design, it does suggest that he is a cause of annoyance to others.

Chara means deception, bunkum. **Chara ni suru** means to wipe off a debt, such as that of gambling, although it does not necessarily mean that the debt is paid. It is just **nakatta-koto ni suru** (treated as if it never existed).

Hora is a large conch shell, used in the old days as a sort of loudspeaker. **Hora wo yū** (to say **hora**) or **fuku** (to blow **hora**) is to exaggerate or to talk big, as in "He said that he caught a fish one meter long yesterday, but that's just **hora**."

One theory is that **charan-poran** is a word synthesized from **chara** and **hora**.

See also Nakatta-koto ni suru, Ocha (wo nigosu), Ōburoshiki.

Chōchin

The Japanese lantern (**chōchin**), a papered-over bamboo frame inside which a candle is lighted, was an indispensable illumination device in the old days.

People of high position and the masters of merchant houses were usually accompanied by attendants (**koshi-ginchaku**) whenever they went out. At night, the attendant carried a lantern ahead to light up the way for his master. At festival time, every house in the community hung lighted lanterns from the eaves to create a gay atmosphere. Sometimes, hundreds of people with lighted lanterns in their hands would stage a celebration parade at night.

From those customs emerged many expressions using the word **chōchin**. **Chōchin-mochi** (lantern bearer) is one who makes a speech in support of a highly placed person or flatters such a person. **Chōchin-kiji** (lantern newspaper article) is a **goma-suri** (toadying) article in favor of someone. **Chōchin wo tsukeru** (light a lantern) is to go along with the majority or the crowd. This last one also refers to the act of following the big operators in their buying and selling on the stock market.

See also Aka-chōchin, Gomasuri.

-Chon (Saka-chon, etc.)

-Chon is used to describe a **tanshin-funin** person who goes to take up a regional post to which he has been assigned, leaving his family behind for reasons such as the schooling of his children. (The number of people who choose **tanshin-funin** because their wives are working still seems to be few.)

The first part of the Korean word *chongak*, which means "bachelor," is adopted and prefixed with the corrupted name of the place to which the person is assigned. For example, **Saka-chon** refers to a person who is assigned to Osaka but left his family behind in, say, Tokyo. **Nago-chon** is "a bachelor in Nagoya," and **Satchon** "a bachelor in Sapporo." It is a word element redolent with the loneliness of the **tanshin-funin**.

See also Shain-ryō, Tanshin-funin.

Chonbo

Many of the games played by people all over the world today originated in China. The most universal are chess (**shōgi** is the Japanese derivative), card games (**hana-garuta** is the Japanese derivative), and mah jongg. We hear that mah jongg is prohibited in the country of its origin, but in Japan there is hardly any male who doesn't know the game. When one steps into the back streets of university districts and business centers, one finds numerous mah jongg parlors. These parlors are important places for forging human relations.

Chonbo is the term used in mah jongg to mean the act of mistakenly declaring that one's hand has been completed when actually it is still incomplete or of completing one's hand by violating the rules. The person guilty of **chonbo** naturally must pay penalties to the other players. (A Western analogy would be the renege or revoke, failing to follow suit in bridge.)

Thus the word means a careless mistake, an oversight. More often than not, it describes an error that is not too serious, usually an amusing blunder. Thus, "He committed another **chonbo**" would have the nuance of "Although he's not bright, he's not the type who makes you despise him." Of course, anyone who repeatedly commits **chonbo** will definitely be regarded as stupid.

Chōrei

At many Japanese factories and offices, the working day begins with **chōrei**. This traditional institution, a source of amazement to Westerners, is something like a morning pep talk.

In some companies, the president gives a brief talk. In large companies, each section holds its own **chōrei,** with the section manager giving the pep talk. At some offices, the workers go through a set of limbering-up exercises and finish off by singing the company song or shouting the company slogan in unison.

The meeting lasts only a few minutes, but it helps create a "let's go" mood and a feeling of identity with the group. **Chōrei** is usually held every morning, but some companies schedule it only for the first day of the week. It's effective in shaking off those Monday morning blues.

See also Shaka, Shaze.

Chotto

In a shop, you want to get the assistant to serve you. In a restaurant, you want to call the waiter's attention. You don't need to feel lost for words. All you have to say is **chotto**. In the street, you want to ask a stranger the way. Your opening gambit can be **chotto**.

For a Japanese, it would be impolite to accost a stranger in the street with **chotto**. But for the visitor from abroad, it is not only acceptable but also somewhat charming if it is said with a sweet, genial, or forlorn demeanor.

For another reason also, **chotto** is one of the first words that anyone coming to Japan from overseas learns. **Chotto matte** is "one moment please" or "wait!" whether on the phone or anywhere else.

See also Sumimasen.

Chotto ippai

On the surface, **chotto ippai** means "let's have a quick drink." It is one of the most frequently heard expressions among company staff members at the end of the day's work, but it does not mean they are alcohol lovers. Sitting down together for a drink after work and before going home for dinner gives salaried workers a chance to exchange information and opinions.

The boss suggests **chotto ippai** to a subordinate when he wants to admonish him privately or to hear his suggestions and complaints. In a way, it's an informal extension of work.

The place chosen for **chotto ippai** is usually an inexpensive drinking establishment. **Chotto ippai,** therefore, is an institution that lubricates human relations among businessmen.

See also Aka-chōchin.

Daikoku-bashira

This is the name of the large central pillar that holds up the entire house. From this, the word takes on the meaning of the central person or thing on whom or which the component members of a family or organization depend.

Daikoku is the Japanese for the Sanskrit word Mahākala, a Buddhist guardian divinity. The popular belief is that it is the guardian divinity of food and the kitchen. Together with **Ebisu** (guardian divinity of commerce), **Daikoku** is one of the Seven Divinities of Good Fortune.

A similar expression is **yatai-bone.** This refers to the framework of the wheeled cart used as an itinerant stall (**yatai**) by vendors of such things as **soba** (buckwheat noodles).

Whereas **daikoku-bashira** is used in a positive sense, such as ''He is that company's **daikoku-bashira**'' and ''The new product we marketed last year has become our company's **daikoku-bashira,**'' **yatai-bone** is used in a negative sense, such as ''That company's **yatai-bone** is loose'' (the company's organization is shaky) or ''That company's **yatai-bone** is not solid'' (the company lacks a mainstay executive or product).

See also Dorubako.

Dame-oshi

Dame-oshi is the name given to the process of making something doubly sure.

You accept an invitation to a business dinner. On the day of the dinner, you get a call from your host's secretary to confirm your attendance. You promise to deliver goods on a certain date. A few days before the scheduled time, the customer inquires if he can still expect delivery on that date. A decision has been reached at a meeting. Some time later, those who attended the meeting are asked to reconfirm the decision.

All these are instances of **dame-oshi.** This kind of reminding and reconfirming sometimes irritates the Westerner, but in Japanese society **dame-oshi** is an accepted practice which ensures that things will go smoothly as previously arranged, decided, or promised. **Dame-oshi** reduces the possibility of last-minute hitches.

Dochira-e?

Very often you will hear Japanese greeting each other on the street with "**Dochira-e?**" which literally means "Where are you going?"

It is not a sign that the Japanese are inquisitive about the destination of someone they happen to meet on the street. It should not be taken as prying into one's private affairs, because it is only a way of greeting, and means no more than a cheery "hello."

If a Japanese is asked "**Dochira-e?**" by an acquaintance, he will not take it for a definite question and will probably just give a vague reply, unless he particularly wants to specify where he is going. When a foreigner is addressed by a Japanese friend on the street, "**Dochira-e?**" he should not feel offended but simply reply with the stock greeting "**chotto soko made**" (just over there) and an ambiguous smile.

Dōki

"How's your business compared with last year?" "Well, in the first half of this year we managed to increase our sales by five percent over **dōki** last year." Here the word means "same period" or "corresponding period," a functional expression that is indispensable in talking about business performance.

"Mr. Yamada is the first among his **dōki** to become a director of the company." Although the word is written with the same Chinese characters as in the first example, it wouldn't make sense if rendered into English as "same period." Used in this sense **dōki** is redolent with meaning. It refers to persons who entered the company in the same year as Mr. Yamada.

This **dōki** relationship is very much emphasized in Japanese organizations where promotion is by seniority and personnel officers make an effort to treat all **dōki** equally in giving promotions or assignments. **Dōki** persons in a company often hold informal meetings of their own to compare notes and maintain contact.

Dokushin-kizoku

This translates literally as "bachelor (or spinster) aristocracy." But do not jump to the conclusion that it refers to a person who has not entered into marriage, the graveyard of life.

Today, because household chores such as cooking, washing, and cleaning are all taken care of by electric appliances, an unmarried man can get by without spending too much time on such chores. He can use his entire salary at his own discretion. He is also free to engage in love affairs.

With a feeling of envy, middle-aged married people gave the name **dokushin-kizoku** to such younger men with time and money at their disposal. Single women salaried workers who are fully enjoying trips overseas and fine meals at good restaurants around town are on the highest rung of this aristocracy.

Of course, once they marry, they no longer belong to this aristocracy. Even while enjoying the aristocratic benefits of being single, many of them have eyes on someone working in the same company as a marriage partner. Aren't they being inconsistent?

See also Sha-nai (kekkon).

Dōmo

Dōmo, which means "very," "much," or "indeed," is a versatile colloquial word. In everyday conversation, it prefaces such words as **arigatō** (thank you) and **sumimasen** (sorry).

When the situation makes it obvious whether

you mean "thank you" or "sorry" or "welcome," the operative word is often dropped and only **dōmo** is used. When repeated in succession, "**dōmo-dōmo**," it has the effect of expressing greater feeling or enthusiasm.

A salesman may introduce himself to a customer with a **dōmo**, have his order book signed and say **dōmo**, and leave with another **dōmo**. The use of **dōmo** alone is not as polite as the full expression **dōmo arigatō**.

Dorubako

The Japanese word for cash box, **kanebako**, is used to mean "a money-maker," "source of revenue," or "financial patron." Nowadays the **kane** (money) in this expression has been replaced by **doru** (dollars). But people never say **yen-bako** or **pound-bako**.

The most profitable business line or product of a company is called its **dorubako**. The expression is used in such ways as "As soon as that company's new product, vitamin X, went on sale, it became the company's **dorubako**" and "The Y Department is our company's biggest **dorubako**."

Dorubako can be used instead of the word "sponsor" in the sentence, "He must have found a **dorubako** or **kane-zuru** (money vine), because he started a new business recently." In this case, the **dorubako** or **kane-zuru** is a wealthy patron who sees potential in a person and furnishes capital for him to get started.

See also Daikoku-bashira.

Dosa-mawari

This refers to the provincial tour of performing artists and theatrical troupes, mostly second-raters. **Dosa** is a code word the underworld in feudal days created by reversing the syllables in "Sado," the island in the Japan Sea to which criminals were sent to serve sentence. Forced labor was so strenuous that prisoners had practically no hope of ever being able to return to the mainland alive. Performers who were perennially touring the provinces had little chance of returning to the cultural center. This was probably the reason the term **dosa-mawari** (touring **dosa**) was applied to them.

It is the custom in big Japanese corporations and the civil service to rotate the assignments of personnel to include stints of a few years in provincial branches or offices. When a person is given successive provincial assignments, he self-deprecatingly says, "My speciality is **dosa-mawari.**"

When a person is assigned to an out-of-the-way place, he is said to have been **tobasareta** (kicked out). In other words, his career course has been interrupted. In Japan workers are rarely dismissed, but this ploy is used to make the worker realize that there is no place for him in the company any more.

See also Jirei, Madogiwa-zoku, Sasen.

Dōsōsei

Old school relationships play an important role in the Japanese business and social world. The simple fact that two businessmen have known each other since college days or even just went to the same school is often enough to open a new account between two firms, expedite contracts, or arrange the informal exchange of business tips otherwise difficult to obtain.

Japanese businessmen therefore go to great pains to maintain their **dōsōsei** (alumni) network. Class reunions are held frequently, and alumni bulletins are circulated to keep the old school ties together. This is an example of a horizontal relationship in Japanese business society, which otherwise tends to be structured vertically.

See also Dōki, Batsu.

Futokoro-gatana

In the English-speaking world, if you should liken a man to a dagger, it is not complimentary. Although the original meaning of **futokoro-gatana** is ''dagger'' or ''dirk,'' it is well-regarded for a person to be described as such in Japan. This is because, in reference to a person, it is used to mean a confidant or a right-hand man.

This meaning comes from the fact that in feudal Japan people carried the dagger in the **futokoro** (bosom). It was an instrument for committing **hara-kiri** in order to defend one's honor.

From this, the word took on today's meaning: a man who is privy to the secret plans of a person holding a responsible position or one who is most trusted by such a person. In other words, the **futokoro-gatana** is a sort of chief of staff and the right hand of a person in high position.

Gaijin

Persons who come from other countries to live in Japan learn very quickly that they are lumped together under the generic name **gaijin** (**gai** = outside, **jin** = person), which they are told means "foreigner." Originally, **gaijin** was used to mean "people outside of one's circle or people with whom one does not have much contact." The people of other countries fell into this category.

During the 200 years of Japan's national isolation up to 1868, the Japanese had contact only with the Chinese and the Dutch. The Chinese were called **tōjin** (citizens of the Tang Dynasty), while the Dutch were called **i-jin,** the character for "**i**" being the one meaning "barbarous," or the one meaning "different"—different color of hair, skin, and eye.

In the twentieth century, foreigners were no longer strangers to the Japanese. The word **i-jin** gave way to **ketō** (hairy **tōjin**), which carried a contemptuous tone and was used by ultra-nationalists. It was after Japan's defeat in World War II that the word **gaijin** came into use. This word has none of the uncomplimentary connotations of previous words used to identify Westerners. **Gaijin** today is used only to mean "non-Japanese," mainly Occidentals.

See also Uchi.

Gakureki

One of the changes taking place in Japanese society today is the attitude toward the **gakureki,** or school background. It used to be that a person's **gakureki** inevitably shaped his course in professional life.

It is only a slight exaggeration to say that, if a person had graduated from the "right" university, his career all the way to the top was just about automatically charted for him. Conversely, no matter how capable, the man who did not come from the "right" school had little chance to reach the top. This fact of life made young men seek a university education in droves.

Today, with more and more people having the benefit of university education, and business having become increasingly competitive, less importance is beginning to be placed on **gakureki**. If he does not have real business ability, a man who comes from a name university can be surpassed by one from a lesser-known institution.

See also Batsu, Dōsōsei.

Gashi-kōkan

For several days after business offices reopen following the New Year holidays, businessmen are busy attending **gashi-kōkan** parties. These are functions at which people gather to exchange New Year's greetings and to ask each other's favor during the coming year. Most of these functions are sponsored by industrial associations. They are usually scheduled during the daytime.

Gashi-kōkan is a very convenient function, because it eliminates the necessity for businessmen to make time-consuming individual rounds to wish each other a happy New Year. It has a very special atmosphere, because participants make determined attempts to meet as many people as possible to exchange greetings.

The function is also known as **meishi-kōkan** which means "exchanging visiting cards." During the period of **gashi-kōkan** parties, businessmen are excused for sitting at their desks flushed with alcohol.

See also Aisatsu-mawari, Meishi.

Gebahyō

Although the standard Japanese–English dictionary gives "rumor" and "gossip" as the English equivalents of **gebahyō,** the Japanese word is usually used with a nuance not contained in the given English equivalents.

It is most frequently used to mean "speculation among outsiders concerning the possible outcome of an event or proceedings, related mostly to personnel matters." Thus, "the **gebahyō** at Kabuto-cho (Japan's Wall Street) is that Mr. A will be selected over Mr. B as the next president of Company X."

The origin of the word goes back to the days when retainers waiting for their lords at the horse-dismounting (**geba**) place outside a castle or a shrine or temple, engaged in idle speculation about personnel changes in the Shogunate government.

Geko

In the old days, affluent families that paid a large amount of tax were known as **jōko,** the first syllable of which is the character meaning "top" or "upper." Its opposite, the word for poor people, was **geko,** the first syllable of which is the character meaning "bottom" or "lower." The **jōko** family possessed a lot of wine casks, but the **geko** family was too poor to have any. Therefore the latter were not able to drink, because they didn't have the wherewithal.

Perhaps in the old days, they teased persons who cannot hold liquor by saying, "You must be too poor (**geko**) to be able to afford a drink." At any rate, nondrinkers and teetotalers are called **geko.**

Heavy drinkers, however, are not called by the opposite term, **jōko.** Robust imbibers are called **hidari-kiki** (left-handed) or **satō** (left-winger). Although one theory is that this way of calling drinkers originated from the fact that the **sake** cup is held in the left hand, it is not substantiated. People who like both sweets and alcohol are known as **ryōtō-zukai** (swordsman who holds swords in both hands), just as the seventeenth-century swordsman Miyamoto Musashi did. But if a person spends too much money on drinking he will become poor (**geko**).

Geta wo azukeru

The **geta** is Japan's indigenous footwear, made of wood and standing about 5 centimeters high. To this day, it is the custom in Japan to remove one's footwear upon entering a house. Until several decades ago, it was even customary to take off the **geta** when entering a theater or a store. The removed **geta** were checked (**azukeru**) with the footgear caretaker in the same way as coats are checked at the entrance of restaurants and theaters today. Once the **geta** has been checked, a person cannot leave the premises without the consent of the other party, in this case the footgear caretaker, because he can't go outside barefooted.

From this custom, **geta wo azukeru** came to mean the act of entrusting to another person's discretion the decision about the action one should take in a situation or leaving the settlement of a matter to another person. **Kimi ni geta wo asuketa** means "You dispose of this matter completely on your responsibility."

Geta wo haku (wear the **geta**) is used to mean "sell a thing at a higher price than the net price" or "put on a margin." This comes from the fact that when one wears the **geta** it is as if he is on stilts.

Giri

Giri is the linchpin of human relations among Japanese. Essentially, the word means the things people must do or the correct way of behavior for smooth social life. Thus it covers a wide range of human attitudes and behavior.

When a person says, "I owe that man **giri**," he means he has received some favor from him at one time and must eventually return the obligation.

To repay a debt of gratitude is **giri wo hatasu.** Sending **ochūgen** (midsummer) and **oseibo** (year-end) gifts, and sending gifts on personal ceremonial occasions, such as coming of age, marriage, or funeral, is one way to **giri wo hatasu.** A person who meticulously observes such practices is praised as **giri-gatai hito** (person who discharges his social duties faithfully). However, if such acts lack sincerity, a person will be criticized as **giri ippen** or doing a thing without heart.

Giri no naka refers to in-law relationships and implies that one must conduct relations with such people as if they were relatives.

In a company, if either a senior and a subordinate or colleagues are in a **giri ga karamu** relationship (bound by **giri**), it means that a **batsu** has been formed.

See also Batsu, Jingi, On.

Go-en

En is a Buddhist term. There is a cause to all things. The medium through which a cause brings about an effect is **en. En** can be expressed in the relationship of past (cause), present (**en**), and future (effect or result).

The relationship between man and woman, social intercourse with neighbors, relations with business partners—all begin with and change with **en,** which in some cases is usually prefixed with the honorific **go.** Thus, **en** is chance or occasion. **En ga aru** means to have a relationship.

When one says, ''We have **en** with that company,'' it means that his company has business transactions with that company or that his company's staff is often present at the same place with the staff of a competing company at a bidding, etc.

In daily life, **en** is often used in reference to the relationship between man and woman. When the parents of a marriageable son or daughter receive an **en no hanashi** or an **endan,** it means someone brings information about a prospective partner for marriage. In such a case, if **en ga aru** (**en** exists), they get married; if **en ga nai** (no **en**), the proposal falls through.

En wo kiru is for a couple to break up.

Gogatsu-byō

In Japan when a young man gains admission to a famous university it is just as if he had obtained a passport to travel along the elite course in his career after graduation. Therefore, the preparation for taking university entrance examinations is gruelling and puts pressure on aspiring young men. When the pressure lifts after successfully hurdling the examinations, many students develop mental and physical disorders. The symptoms usually come out in May (**gogatsu**), one month after the new school year starts. The ailment is known, therefore, as **gogatsu-byō** (May sickness).

In recent years, this phenomenon has been observed also among graduates who have just obtained employment and started working in April. Some are afflicted so heavily with **gogatsu-byō** that they resign after only two or three months. Some even commit suicide.

These are young men who believed that the aim in life is to enter a famous university or a leading corporation. Once they attain the aim, lethargy sets in, and all the people around them appear to have greater ability than they. This probably causes neurosis. **Gogatsu-byō** is most prevalent among serious-minded youth. A little bit of frivolity may be the antidote for **gogatsu-byō.**

Gokurō-sama, Otsukare-sama

The word **gokurō-sama** means "I appreciate your labor," "Thank you for your trouble," or sometimes "I sympathize with you for your tough assignment." When the word is said to someone going off to attend to a task, it can carry the meaning of "Good luck!" Thus it can be said to a person who is setting off for work, who is in the process of performing a task, or who has finished a job or returned from work.

Otsukare-sama is said to a person who has completed a job. It means "It must have been tiring" and expresses gratitude. The businessman returning home from work is greeted by his wife with **otsukare-sama** or **gokurō-sama.**

See also Shitsurei shimasu.

Gomasuri

You find him in every organization and every society. He may not be a bad fellow, but his colleagues do not speak well of him. More often than not, he is usually looked upon with contempt by all but the person on whom he practices his technique.

In the English-speaking world, the **gomasuri** is known as the "apple-polisher." A high-sounding name for him is "sycophant," a self-seeking person who courts favor in a servile manner by flattering others. The literal translation of the Japanese word is "a person who grinds sesame seeds."

Roasted sesame seeds are ground in an earthenware mortar to make flavoring for Japanese-style dishes. In the grinding process, the seeds fly in all directions and stick to the wall of the mortar almost in a cringing way.

Thus, the noun **gomasuri**—apple polisher or apple polishing—and the verb **goma wo suru**—to flatter or toady, figuratively, of course.

Goshūgi

One of the characteristics of Japanese society is the way people observe formalities and conventions, some of which might appear irrational to the Western mind. One of these is **goshūgi. Go** is an honorific prefix and **shūgi** means "celebration or congratulation."

This is carried over into the business world when one gives a **goshūgi torihiki** or when we have a **goshūgi sōba.** The former is a transaction made not because of its business merits but in order to express congratulations to a person or company just starting a business.

The latter is generally used to describe the buoyant prices on the stock exchange on the first business day of the New Year. New Year's is a felicitous time, and it just won't do to have a slumping market, no matter what the realities. Thus, buyers and sellers usually cooperate to give the market a boost when it reopens for business after the New Year holidays.

Gyōsha

The components of this word are **gyō,** which means "trade, business, profession," and **sha,** which means "man, person, party." The word is used primarily to differentiate business enterprises from government agencies and nonprofit organizations and carries a rather slighting connotation.

In Japan's feudal days, merchants were on the bottom rung of the social ladder. They were regarded as cunning, deceitful, and mindful only of making a profit, much the same as in the West. At the opening of the twentieth century, merchants who dealt with the government began to be called **gyōsha,** with the nuance that they are "a breed that cannot be trusted."

Today, in the eyes of government agencies even the most respectable big corporations are **gyōsha.** The big corporations call their subcontractors **gyōsha.** The subcontractors, in their turn, regard *their* subcontractors as their **gyōsha.** This goes on down the line all the way to trifle merchants.

When the word is prefixed with **dō** (meaning "same"), the unpleasant nuance disappears; it simply means "a company in the same field of business"—**dō-gyōsha.**

Hada

Hada is skin, but in Japanese expressions it is not only used in its base meaning, but also to mean temperament, character, disposition, bent, type, mold, etc.

Hada-zawari means feel or touch, as in soft or rough touch. In reference to a person, we say **hada-zawari ga yawarakai** (soft). This means that the person is gentle-mannered, affable, courteous.

Hada ni awanai is "not suitable or agreeable to the skin." It is a polite way of saying that one doesn't like a certain person. It also means that two persons are not compatible with each other or cannot get along with each other because of personality, ideology, taste, or interests. If someone feels uncomfortable in a certain post because it doesn't suit his temperament, he can say that it's a **hada ni awanai** position for him. This would mean that he feels like a fish out of water. The opposite is **hada ni au** (*see* Ki [ni iru]).

When one wants to say a certain person is a scholarly type or has an academic bent, the expression **hada** is also used. The statement would be "he is **gakusha-hada**." **Gakusha** (scholar) can be replaced with politician (**seiji-ka**), merchant (**shō-nin**), scientist (**kagaku-sha**), diplomat (**gaikōkan**), artist (**geijutsa-ka**), etc.

Haenuki

This is the term applied to a person who was born and brought up in the same place or a person who entered a company upon graduation from school and has ever since remained in the same company. In other words, a purebred. The word is used in such ways as "He is our company's **haenuki** accountant."

A word with a similar meaning is **kissui**, which

means pure and unalloyed. In the sample sentence given above, the word **kissui** could be substituted for **haenuki.** The difference in nuance is that in the case of **haenuki** the stress is on the fact that he has never changed companies, whereas **kissui** connotes that his occupational classification has never changed.

The contrasting words are **tozama** and **amakudari.** A **tozama** coming into a company where **kissui** and **haenuki** form the nucleus of the staff finds it extremely difficult to get assimilated.

See also Ama-kudari, Kogai, Tozama.

Hai and Ie

Hai is yes and **ie** is no. That sounds simple. However, unfortunately for international communications, the Japanese **hai** does not always have the same meaning as the English "yes." To the question "He does not speak Japanese, does he?" the Japanese answer "**hai**" would mean the same as the English answer "no," and vice versa.

The Japanese often carry over into English their peculiar usage of **hai** and **ie,** causing misunderstanding and confusion. Another problem that arises in connection with **ie** is that the Japanese tend to avoid using it. They don't want to embarrass or hurt the other party by refuting, denying, or rejecting.

The safest way for the foreign businessman dealing with Japanese is not to accept a "yes" or a "no" as an answer but to persuade them to phrase the answer in a sentence.

Hame wo hazusu

There are two theories as to the source of this expression. One is that **hame** is the corrupted pronunciation of **hami,** which means the horse's bit. The other is that **hame** stands for a board fence. If the bit is removed (**hazusu**), the horse will no longer be restrained and will be free to move around at will. If the fence is removed, one will no longer be confined. The expression therefore means "pull out all the stops."

Every communal society has a safety valve mechanism in the form of periodic festivals or feast days at which the people **hame wo hazusu** and indulge in unrestrained merrymaking, casting aside for a moment all the strict values that keep them bound at ordinary times. This letting off of steam is necessary in order to maintain society on an even keel and to sustain production activities.

One instance of **hame wo hazusu** in Japanese business society is the **bureikō** party. Even ordinarily serious and conservative corporate employees are expected to **hame wo hazusu** from time to time. If one doesn't know how to **hame wo hazusu,** he will be shunned by his colleagues.

See also Bureikō.

Hana

The Japanese word for flower (**hana**) is used, as in the case of the English word, to describe the brilliant, the decorative, or the pride of something.

Kinjō ni hana wo soeru means "to add luster to what is already brilliant," or additional honor or fame. **Hana wo motaseru** (literally, let the other person hold the flower) is to give the credit to another person. This expression, however, can sometimes carry the ironic nuance of "let him have the flower, but not the fruit."

Young female office workers are called **shokuba no hana** (flower of the work place), which has a double meaning. One is that they are a refreshing presence, and the other is that they are wallflowers who cannot be expected to contribute substantially to actual work.

In the world of Kabuki drama, there is the **hana-michi** (literally, flower way), a stage-high narrow, elevated pathway that leads from the main stage through the midst of the audience to the back of the theater. The star of a play enters or exits from the stage over this pathway with great flourish. This was adopted to describe a corporate president's retirement in a blaze of glory as **hana-michi wo kazaru**. When his juniors prepare such a stage for his retirement, it is **hana-michi wo tsukutte ageru**.

Hanko

Without this instrument, which is slightly thicker than a pencil and about five centimeters long, business in Japan would quickly come to a standstill. The **hanko,** or seal, is used in place of one's personal signature.

Most corporate decisions must await the completion of the process whereby documents have been read and approved, then stamped with the **hanko** of all those concerned. This process rarely results in hasty decisions. The seal businessmen use in signing routine papers is usually a **san·mon-ban,** which is ready-made and available at stationery stores.

Hanko is shortened to **han** and is sometimes pronounced **ban** when used in combination with another word, such as **san·mon-ban.**

See also Ringi.

Hara

Anatomically, **hara** is the abdomen or stomach. Used in figures of speech, the word can mean the heart or the mind of a man, but not of a woman. **Hara** appears in a large number of expressions.

The author who devoted a whole book to **hara-gei** (stomach art) would probably say that it is presumptuous to try to explain in just a few lines this Japanese problem-solving technique. **Hara-gei** may be explained as a technique for solving a problem through negotiation between two individuals without the use of direct words. You don't reveal to the other party what is in your **hara,** but you unmistakably and effectively communicate your purpose, desire, demand, intention, advice, or whatever through **hara-gei.**

To do this, you bring into play psychology, intuition, and your knowledge of the other party's personality, background, ambitions, personal connections, etc., and also what the other party knows about you. Only people with plenty of experience and cool nerves can make it succeed, but a lot of communication between Japanese in high positions is through **hara-gei** (*see* Ishin-denshin).

Hara wo watte hanasu (to cut open the stomach and talk) = to have a heart-to-heart talk.

Hara wo miseru (to show the stomach) = to reveal what is in one's mind.

Hara wo kukuru (to bundle up the stomach) = to become resigned to something or resolve to do something, whatever the outcome.

Hara-guroi (the stomach is black) = a treacherous person, a schemer.

Seppuku = to cut open the stomach. **Puku** is another way of reading the character for **hara.** This is the proper word for the act which has become known in the outside world as **hara-kiri. Seppuku** was the honorable course given to the feudal warrior in place of execution. It is an act whose purpose is to show that one's **hara** is clean.

See also Futokoro gatana.

Tsume-bara wo kiru means **seppuku** which one does not want to do but cannot avoid. When the people around a person conspire to place that person in a situation where he just has to **seppuku,** it is called **tsume-bara wo kiraseru.** This expression is used in contemporary society when a person is forced into a position where he has no recourse but to resign from his post or organization.

Jibara wo kiru (to cut one's own stomach) = to pay for something out of one's own pocket.

Hara-no-mushi

In the Japanese language, there are many expressions which seem to indicate that the Japanese people have various kinds of worms (**mushi**) in their stomach (**hara**). One such worm has the power of prescience and tells a person that he will be promoted or sent on an assignment abroad or will lose a contract, etc. This is **mushi ga shiraseru,** and it is like being told by one's sixth sense about a future happening. When one is in a bad mood for no particular reason, the worm in his stomach is not in its proper place (**mushi no idokoro ga warui**).

If you don't know why but you just don't like a certain person instinctively, it is because **mushi ga sukanai** (worm does not like). When one suffers a loss and there is nothing he an do about it, his **hara no mushi ga osamaranai** (worm in the stomach does not calm down), or he just can't get over it. When a baby has fits or a severe stomach ache, it is because **kan no mushi** (worm in the spleen) is acting violently.

Because the tensions of modern society have increased the symptoms of stress, these expressions are heard very often.

See also Hara, Ki.

Hashigo

In the West, when one talks about the ladder (**hashigo**) in corporate life, it means the promotion ladder.

One cannot always rejoice just because he has climbed the ladder. Once upstairs, the ladder might be removed (**hashigo wo hazusareru**). This means that a person has been given a ranking post but has no subordinates. Having no organization to work for him, his influence is bottled up and his effectiveness in the company nullified.

In the life of the Japanese businessman the word

hashigo is heard more often in another context. This is **hashigo-zake,** literally "ladder **sake."** It is an indispensable institution in Japanese business society. After the day's work, Japanese corporate workers go drinking in groups, usually starting at an **aka-chōchin.** After a few drinks, they move on to another drinking establishment.

Because many people do not reveal their **hon-ne** until after substantial doses of alcohol have loosened them up, the group moves on to still another bar. The senior man in the group foots the bill. For him this is a painful, unofficial duty that goes with the higher post he holds.

See also Aka-chōchin, Hon-ne.

Heso wo mageru

The navel and the cowlick of the hair are normally centrally located. A person who is odd, perverse, intractable, or cantankerous is described as **heso-magari** (out-of-line navel) or **tsumuji-magari** (off-center cowlick).

Heso wo mageru (make the navel out of line) and **tsumuji wo mageru** (make the cowlick off-center) are the verb forms, meaning to get angry, act perverse, or be spiteful without a justifiable cause. Although a person who "puts his navel out of line" may not have a justifiable reason for doing so, in many cases he has an underlying reason, such as being left out of a thing or having been made to lose face.

A **heso-magari** is usually rather a petty person who is not manly. But subordinates have to be careful not to push their boss into a position where his navel becomes out of line, because then they will be the ones to suffer.

Hidari-uchiwa

The samurai of feudal days were constantly on the alert against surprise attacks and always kept their right hand free so that they could make a quick grab for their sword. Thus, to cool himself in the hot summer, he used a fan (**uchiwa**) with his left (**hidari**) hand. From this, **hidari-uchiwa** came to mean "be prepared for the unexpected," "have something in reserve," then "have presence of mind, composure," and finally "to live without worries, comfortably."

Thus, it is the dream of all Japanese salaried workers to achieve the state of **hidari-uchiwa**—a life of comfort and ease, with a house of his own, sufficient money in the bank, pension, children all grown up, and no worries of any kind.

There is another word that also means fan: **sensu.** The difference between **uchiwa** and **sensu** is that the former is the word for the fan people used when relaxing at home, whereas the latter is the one they carried with them when going out, because **sensu** is collapsible.

See also Teinen.

Hijikake-isu

When you walk into a Japanese office, you can tell who outranks whom by noticing the type of chairs they are sitting in. The chair most coveted by company employees is the **hijikake-isu,** a large one with armrests. The rank-and-file sit in the simplest of functional office chairs. They are chairs not for resting but for working.

When a person is promoted to the first rung of the managerial ladder, he gets a chair with an armrest and quite often a bigger desk. As he goes up the ladder, he is given an increasingly larger and more comfortable **hijikake-isu.** When he gets to a leather-upholstered chair with high back rest, he is a director or perhaps the president. It's a chair for sitting back and thinking.

Hikinuki

In the Japanese corporation, the recruiting of personnel is, as a rule, conducted only once a year when young men graduate from the universities or high schools in spring. Persons who have worked in other companies are not usually hired. The exception is **ama-kudari,** a system under which companies take in retiring government officials to fill executive posts.

However, on the rare occasion when a company urgently needs a person with a highly specialized talent or experience, it scouts other organizations to find a suitable man to persuade to change jobs. This is called **hikinuki,** literally "to extract" or "to pluck out."

See also Ama-kudari, Teiki-sayō.

Hi-no-kuruma

Hi-no-kuruma is the fiery (**hi**) car (**kuruma**) of the Buddhist hell used to transport dead sinners. To be transported in such a way is excruciating. Because financial distress is just as painful, it is described as being like a **hi-no-kuruma.**

The term is used for any case of financial distress, whether it be that of the government, a company, a family, or an individual. It is used for situations in which the safe or the purse is empty.

Financial difficulties are also expressed metaphorically by reference to another kind of **kuruma,** the word for vehicles that run on wheels. The character for **kuruma** is pronounced **sha** when prefixed with characters that indicate the type of vehicle: **jidōsha** (automobile), **jitensha** (bicycle), etc. A company in a state of **jitensha-sōgyō,** literally "bicycle operation," is existing hand-to-mouth and is just barely managing to get along without going bankrupt. This comes from the fact that the bicycle would fall on its side if it stops running. Which situation is worse, **hi-no-kuruma** or **jitensha-sōgyō?** It is hard to say, but probably it is **hi-no-kuruma.**

Hiru-andon

Hiru-andon translates as "a lamp in broad daylight." In broad daylight one cannot tell whether a lamp has been lit or not. From this fact, the word is used to refer to a person whose presence or existence is not regarded as important or to describe a person when it is difficult to determine whether he has value or not. However, it does not mean a person who is slow to react (such a person is called **keikōtō** = fluorescent lamp, which takes time to light up) or is mediocre.

In many cases a Japanese organization operates better when its head is a person who does not stand out but who has a **kiremono** (sharp and able man) as his **futokoro-gatana** or chief of staff. In such a case, the top man is a symbol and the deputy or chief of staff holds the responsibility. Often there are two or more deputies and/or staff officers, so power does not become concentrated in one person. Perhaps this perception of the organization, which has existed in Japan since the old days, has prevented the emergence of a dictator.

Consequently, **hiru-andon** is not necessarily a deprecating reference, and **kiremono** is not necessarily a word of praise.

See also Futokoro-gatana.

Hitori-zumō

Together with **jūdō, sumō** is a traditional national sport of the Japanese people. As a professional sport **sumō** enjoys tremendous popularity today as in the old days.

In recent years, the number of foreign **sumō** fans has increased greatly, and the presentation of a trophy to the winner of each of the six annual tournaments by an American airline company, whose representative gives a congratulatory speech, has become a popular feature.

Sumō is a contest between two wrestlers. If one contestant is overwhelmingly the stronger, we say **sumō ni naranai** (it doesn't make a **sumō** match) which means "it's no match." If, even in such a hopeless match, the weaker contestant puts everything into charging at his opponent, he is said to be "having a **sumō** match by himself" (**hitori-zumō wo totte-iru**).

This last expression is used also to describe a person who is tackling an extremely difficult task all by himself without being able to get anyone to co-operate with him. The person is so earnest that it is almost tragic, and at the same time comic. Instead of sympathizing with him, the others think he is pitiful, saying, "Since he can't get coopera-tion, he should abandon it." (Yet, nobody is moved to lend a helping hand!)

Hiya-meshi-kui

Rice, as everyone knows, is the Japanese staple. It is eaten boiled and unflavored. It tastes best when eaten warm. In Japan's predemocratic days, it was the privilege of the head of the family and the el-dest son to eat just-cooked warm rice. All other members of the family sometimes had to be satis-fied with rice that had become cold. Those were the **hiya-meshi-kui**—literally, "cold rice eaters."

With the democratization of the Japanese family in the past generation or so, the people are not so fussy today as to who in the family gets to eat warm rice. But the term **hiya-meshi-kui** has been adopted in the working world of men—in business and the government bureaucracy—to refer to per-sons in unimportant or insignificant positions. Per-sons who are lagging behind in the promotion race think they are being forced to eat **hiya-meshi.**

The **madogiwa-zoku** are, in a way, similar to the **hiya-meshi-kui,** to the extent that both are given the cold treatment. The word **madogiwa-zoku** has a "sunny side" feeling, whereas **hiya-meshi-kui** has the feeling of being in the "shadow." Of course, if circumstances should change, both may, happily, get back into the mainstream.

See also Madogiwa-zoku.

Hon•ne and Tatemae

"That man doesn't disclose his **hon•ne** (real intentions) easily" is an expression Japanese businessmen use when talking about a tough negotiator on the other side. Your counterpart in a business negotiation may be obstinate not because he wants to be, but because, under certain circumstances, he has to emphasize his company's **tatemae** (principles or official stance).

When the **tatemae** and the **hon•ne** are the same, there is no problem. But sometimes it happens that they are at variance with each other. The negotiation then becomes an exercise in trying to find a way to satisfy the **hon•ne** without compromising the **tatemae,** at least on the surface.

Excessive adherence to **tatemae,** of course, is often used as a ploy to gain a better bargaining position. The reluctance to reveal the **hon•ne** and the tendency to stick ostensibly to **tatemae** also occur in private social relations, especially when the **hon•ne** is not very laudable.

Ippai kū

In ordinary use, this expression means "to eat (**kū**) a lot or a stomachful (**ippai**)." But **ippai kutta** (ate a stomachful) is used synonymously with "I was tricked (outwitted, bamboozled)." These meanings come from the practice of making the other party trust you by first treating him generously to drinks and food and then, when he is off his guard, to trick him.

It is, in a way, a confidence game. It is because the person treated, too, has some underlying motive that in the end he has **ippai kutta.** As in the expression "trying to outfox each other," both parties are not above board, and it is hard to choose between them. If one should swear, "Confound him! He put one over on me," people will derisively smile in their hearts. "It was a case of two bad fellows trying to outfox each other. The one who lost out is the fool."

The word **ippai** also appears in the conversation: "How about **ippai**?" Here, **ippai** refers to "a cup of **sake**," and the suggestion means "Let's have a chat while drinking **sake** at an **aka-chōchin** or some such place." Although their intention may be just **ippai** (one cup), they usually end up by drinking **ippai** (much, a great deal), and become **gozen-sama** (a person who returns home in the wee hours).

See also Aka-chōchin.

Irasshai-mase

When people from another country come to Japan, they soon learn even without being taught that

irasshai-mase must mean "welcome." This is because whenever they walk into a shop, a restaurant, a theater, a bank, a friend's home, etc., they are invariably greeted with this word. In fact, in some establishments it seems as if the only duty of the person stationed at the entrance is to bow and utter this word. If they browse through a department store, they will hear the word dozens of times, because clerks of each section greet the shopper as he/she enters their territory.

Banks and department stores train their staff in the manner of saying **irasshai-mase**—politely, deferentially, and with an affable smile. It is said in much the same spirit as "may I help you" in English-speaking countries, to put the customer at ease.

At such places as the fish store, the grocery, and **sushi** shops, which feature fresh food, the greeting is shortened to the spirited "**rasshai!**" Barkers, too, use the corrupted form. In their case, the meaning is not so much "welcome" but "step right up."

Iroke

The suffix **ke** is used to indicate a slight tinge to the state denoted by the main part of the word. **Iroke** limits the meaning of the **iro** (explained in the next entry) to shape, appearance, and love. "**Iroke ga dete kita** (literally, a tinge of color has emerged) recently in the girl next door" would mean that she has grown to the stage where men notice her physical attributes. **Iroke-zuku** has the same meaning, but it has a rather coarse ring and is used jeeringly to intimate that the girl has become conscious of the opposite sex.

In the expression **iroke wo miseru** (show or reveal **iroke**), **iroke** means "desire, inclination, interest." Thus, "He shows **iroke** for this transaction" and "When he was approached to switch jobs, he showed **iroke**."

Corporate employees are always showing **iroke** for promotion, but if it is done too glaringly they will be teased: "He is **iroke tappuri** (full of desire) for the manager's post." **Iroke tappuri** is also used scornfully of a woman past her prime who tries to look young with the help of cosmetics and youngish clothing.

Iro wo tsukeru

Iro basically stands for color or hue, but the word is used in a great variety of meanings, including good form, beautiful shape, good appearance, etc. Thus, a handsome man (**otoko**) is known as **iro-otoko**. Because women usually prefer an **iro-otoko** as their partner in a love affair, the word **iro** by itself has become to be used to mean love.

"She is the **iro** of Mr. Y" would mean that the girl is Mr. Y's lover or sweetheart. **Iro-gonomi** is a person who likes (**gonomi**) to have affairs (**iro-goto**). A playboy would be called **iro-goto-shi**.

The feelings of love and liking are accompanied by compassion and consideration. Thus, **iro wo tsukeru** (apply color) means to give special consideration. When the wage bargaining between management and the union nears a climax, the company president would say, "We understand your position, so we'll **iro wo tsukeru** by ___ yen," meaning that the company would give an additional ___ yen in raise.

In most cases, however, the expression is used informally. The boss tells his subordinate, "I have **iro wo tsukete oita-yo** on your next bonus," meaning "I've fixed it so that you'll get a little extra on your next bonus." This is a useful gimmick in handling subordinates.

See also Shuntō.

Ishibashi wo tataku

This means tap (**tataku**) the stone bridge (**ishibashi**), and it carries the meaning of "look before you leap." The stone bridge is more solid than the wooden bridge and is generally regarded as being so strong that it would not crumble easily. But the overly careful person would tap it before venturing to cross it in order to make doubly sure that there is no danger of its crumbling under his weight.

Thus this expression is used to describe people who are exceptionally cautious. If a person's cautiousness borders on timidity, he is ridiculed as a person who will not cross the stone bridge even after tapping it to test its strength (**Kare wa ishibashi wo tataitemo wataranai**).

At times the businessman will be required to have the prudence of the man who won't cross a stone bridge even after tapping it as well as the daring spirit to take resolute action.

It is often said that the majority of Japanese business executives are of the type who tap the stone bridge, while many among the foot soldiers of business are daring men of action. In the frontier growth industries, however, the number of daring executives is increasing.

Ishin-denshin

Ishin-denshin is communication of thought without the medium of words. The expression means "what the mind thinks, the heart transmits." In other societies, particularly Western, communication generally has to be expressed in specific words to be thoroughly understood. To the Westerner, therefore, the Japanese sometimes seem to have telepathic powers, because so often communication among Japanese is achieved without the use of words.

This is because the many formalities, conventions and common standards developed in a society that gives priority to harmonious relations make it easy to understand what goes on in the mind of the other peson.

The younger generation of Japanese who have become more individualistic are losing the **ishin-denshin** faculty.

See also Hara(-gei).

Jihyō

In Japan, because of the lifetime employment system, employees generally do not resign from a company. Resignation is usually regarded as a very grave matter. When a person wishes to quit a company, he must submit a **jihyō**—a formal letter of resignation. An intent to resign transmitted verbally has no force and is completely disregarded.

It happens quite often that the management refuses to accept a **jihyō,** although it has no legal power to prevent an employee from quitting. However, in the Japanese social climate, which demands a harmonious solution to everything, it is socially difficult for the employee to quit his job unless the management agrees to let him go. If agreement is given, it becomes **en·man-taisha**—leaving a company in an amicable manner.

Jingi

The five virtues as taught by Confucius are benevolence, righteousness, propriety, wisdom, and sincerity. **Jingi** stands for the first two. Mencius taught that **jin** (humanity, benevolence) and **gi** (justice, righteousness) are the basic principles of morality. These teachings crossed over into Japan, and the samurai society adopted **jingi** as the ethical code for maintaining social order.

As time passed, the underworld adopted the word **jingi,** which it used to mean the principles governing the relationship between the boss and his henchmen. The underworld created the term **jingi wo kiru** (to cut **jingi**) to mean their style of self-introduction using special gestures and verbal expressions. From this, the term took on the meaning of "following a prescribed procedure to pay one's respects."

Thus, a company starting a new line of business will **jingi wo kiru** to companies already in that field to avoid excessive competition. The same procedure is followed when a company recruits personnel from another company in the same line of business.

In this respect, **jingi wo kiru** has a meaning somewhat similar to **nemawashi,** but because the word smacks of the underworld, it is not used on formal occasions.

See also Nemawashi.

Jinji-idō

March is a month of anxious expectation for workers in the Japanese corporate world, because most companies and government offices carry out their annual large-scale staff reassignments (**jinji-idō**) before the new fiscal year starts in April. (Minor changes are made around October also.)

Periodic job rotation of personnel at all levels is a common practice in Japan. It is a system for developing human resources—a versatile staff capable of undertaking a wide variety of tasks and a managerial class with a companywide outlook.

At the middle management level, certain posts are considered as stepping stones to executive positions. Thus, under the Japanese seniority system, persons who reach an age that qualifies them for such key posts become particularly anxious, because the next **jinji-idō** may determine the rest of their career in the company. **Jinji-idō** is an important event for outsiders, too, because it directly affects their contacts in the company.

Jin-myaku

This is a newly coined word not found in dictionaries, but it is widely used in all walks of life, because it aptly expresses one of the vital factors of Japanese life. **Jin** means "man, person, human being," and **myaku** means "vein," as in a vein of mineral deposits. The closest English equivalent is "personal connections."

The Japanese are cool toward people they don't know. But it is easy to thaw any Japanese if you know his **jin-myaku.** An introduction from anyone in his **jin-myaku** works like magic, swiftly and easily opening doors that reason, persuasion, or argument could not pry open.

The building up of **jin-myaku** is a lifetime process, beginning in one's school days. A large **jin-myaku** is probably the biggest asset of the Japanese businessman, because human relationships are of paramount importance in Japanese society.

See also Dōki, Batsu.

Jirei

Jirei is a piece of paper that brings joy or dismay to Japanese working in companies or government offices. Usually just a couple of lines on a single sheet of paper, the **jirei** notifies an individual that he has been employed, promoted, demoted, transferred, reassigned, dismissed, or retired. The wording is usually expressed as an order. No personnel changes are carried out without a **jirei.**

Spring is the season of the **jirei,** because it is the time when recruits fresh out of college are employed en masse and organizations carry out a wholesale reshuffle of assignments. Once a **jirei** is issued, there is no chance of its being withdrawn.

There is, however, one type of **jirei** that is not final. It is the **shimbun** (newspaper) **jirei,** the name given cynically to newspaper reports of pending appointments of top-level personnel.

See also Jinji-ido.

Kaban-mochi

This is the person who carries (**mochi** = person who holds) the boss's briefcase (**kaban**) and accompanies him everywhere on his business calls. In a way, he appears to be the counterpart of the European and American secretary. Unlike the Western secretary, however, the **kaban-mochi** is not necessarily a competent person. Usually, his ability doesn't go much beyond the ability to carry a briefcase and to cater to the boss's whims.

Thus, when someone says, ''That fellow is Mr. A's **kaban-mochi,**'' there is a tone of contempt and, perhaps, of envy. There are many expressions of this sort which sarcastically and enviously describe a person who has no ability but is treated like an aide by the boss just because he knows how to fawn. They include **chabōzu** and **koshi-ginchaku.**

Koshi-ginchaku is the moneybag or pouch for

carrying small articles that people in the old days strung from their waist—something like the pouchette carried by today's fashionable girls. Because it is always hanging on to a person, **koshiginchaku** was adopted to refer to one who is always following right behind an important person, as if dangling from him.

See also Gomasuri, Cha-bōzu.

Kabu ga agaru

This expression has the same meaning as the English "his stock rises" and is used in exactly the same way. Employed as a metaphor, it means one's stock rises or one's public esteem goes up, or one gains in stature. The reverse is **kabu ga sagaru,** or "his stock falls."

In Japanese society, where human relations and reputation among one's fellows are of the utmost importance, these two terms are heard very often and can have far-reaching consequences for the persons so described. Thus, there is a doomsday sound to **kabu ga sagaru.**

Kachō, Kasei

The organization of a Japanese business corporation is generally division-department-section. In most cases, the section is known as **ka.** Literally translated, **kasei** means "section system."

Kasei is also used to refer to the fact that the **ka** is the level at which all routine business is dispatched. The section manager, known as **kachō,**

therefore, holds an important position in the middle management of Japanese firms. He is the key man, around forty years of age, who makes all the routine business decisions and supervises the implementation of those decisions. Special project teams and groups are also usually organized at the level of **ka.**

A word of warning: In the Ministry of International Trade and Industry, the majority of **ka** are known in English as "division" and a few as "section."

See also Buchō.

Kachū-no-kuri

Translated directly, this means "chestnuts in the fire." Having its source in Aesop's fables, **kachū-no-kuri wo hirou** is exactly the same as the English "to pull somebody's chestnuts out of the fire."

Aesop's fables were brought into Japan in the late sixteenth century by Jesuit missionaries. Even during the period when Japan was closed to the outside world for two and a half centuries, the fables enjoyed popularity among the people and became the source of expressions that are the same in Japan and the West: **tora-no-i wo karu kitsune** (a fox in lion's skin), **suppai budō** (sour grapes). In the case of **kachū-no-kuri,** many Japanese are not aware that it came from the West, because there is a similar scene in the old Japanese folk tale "**Saru-kani-kassen,**" a story about a crab that defeats a monkey with the help of a chestnut.

A proverb relating to taking a risk is **koketsu-ni-**

irazumba koji wo ezu (unless you go into the tiger's lair, you will not be able to capture a tiger cub). The source of this is China. It refers to the risk one takes in one's own interest and is different from pulling another person's chestnuts out of the fire.

See also Tora(-no-ko).

Kai

Kai has existed in the Japanese language since ancient times and means "effective, fruitful."

Iki-gai expresses the thought of "joy of living" and "worthwhileness of life" and is thus used in such sentences as "My present work is my **iki-gai**" and "I have a grandson now, so I've found an **iki-gai** for my old age."

Kaishō-nashi means good-for-nothing, undependable, and useless. It is therefore used to express scorn. An entrepreneur who lets his company go bankrupt will be denounced by his employees as "this **kaishō-nashi!**" The husband who spends all his time drinking and gambling will be abused by his wife with the same words.

Kaigai-shii is the adjective to describe one who is working with lots of spirit and life, one who is lively and energetic. **Kaishō,** more often than not, is used by a person of lower rank in referring to a superior, whereas **kaigai-shii** is generally used by a superior to praise someone under him. If a company is blessed with a president who possesses **kaishō** and employees who work **kaigai-shiku,** it is sure to prosper.

Kaigi

Some students of the Japanese style of management say that consensus formation takes the place of the process known in other countries as decision-making. **Kaigi** is a meeting or conference held to discuss problems and eventually to reach a consensus.

The meeting may be of members of the same department or of representatives of several departments. **Kaigi** is also a meeting with representatives of outside organizations. Some Japanese executives complain that there are too many **kaigi** in their business life; they believe that intra-office telephone calls, memos, and the distribution of reports could take the place of many of the meetings.

A foreign businessman calling on a Japanese executive to discuss some matter informally is already in **kaigi** with his counterpart's colleagues and aides, even if the foreigner does not realize it, because the matter will be brought up at an intra-office **kaigi** afterward.

Kaki-ire-doki

Every year shops and department stores in Japan have two **kaki-ire-doki**—the traditional gift-giving seasons in midsummer and December. This is a term used to mean "the season when earnings are big" or "raking-in time."

Literally translated the Chinese characters mean "time to write in." Some dictionaries explain the meaning as "the period when merchants are kept busy writing their sales into the ledger." The origin of the word, however, is not so cheerful. Originally it meant "put up as security" and came from writing in (**kaki-ire**) on an IOU the item put up as collateral for a loan.

Over the years, the way the term was used underwent changes, until it eventually assumed its current meaning. The term, of course, is not limited to describing the rush season for retailers. Other kinds of business may have their own **kaki-ire-doki.**

See also Nippachi.

Kaki-kyūka

Kaki-kyūka means summer vacation. Although still not on the scale of European countries, **kaki-kyūka** has become in recent years an established institution for corporate employees in Japan, too. It has become customary for an entire factory to shut down for a week or so during the hottest period, while the office staff adjust their schedules to take their vacation alternately. Many companies even urge their employees to take part of their annual leave during July and August in addition to the special **kaki-kyūka.**

The businessman uses the summer vacation as a time to make his family happy, with a visit to seaside or mountain resorts to escape from the oppressive heat and humidity of the Japanese summer.

See also Yūkyū-kyūka.

Kakushi-gei

Japanese businessmen are all expected to have a **kakushi-gei,** literally, a hidden talent. The talent referred to, however, has nothing directly to do with business or managerial ability. It refers to singing, playing a musical instrument, reciting, mimicking, parlor stunts, magic tricks, or any such amateur entertaining ability.

At office parties, every person attending is called upon to display his **kakushi-gei.** On such an occasion, if you really have a hidden talent nobody knew about, you create a good impression. Those who don't have any usually sing a currently popular song or a tune they learned long ago. This custom of having everybody contribute to the entertainment helps not only to liven up a party but also to build up camaraderie.

When parties are given for clients, some really talented persons on the host's side are called upon to demonstrate their **kakushi-gei.** Not a few corporate employees spend some of their free time polishing a performance expressly for use at parties.

See also Ohako, Kangei-kai, Bōnen-kai.

Kamatoto

This is a hybrid word made up of the first part of the word **kamaboko** and **toto,** baby talk for fish. **Kamaboko** is a sort of preserved food made from boiled fish paste. One might say it is the Japanese counterpart of the Western sausage. Anyway, every child knows what it is.

Thus, it would be out of character if a grown woman should ask, "Is **kamaboko** really made from **ototo?**" She is just pretending that she doesn't know and thus is trying to act cute.

So, a woman who knows but feigns ignorance (especially about relations between the sexes) is called a **kamatoto.** If such a woman is close to forty in age, the comment becomes a bit caustic, and the word used is **kamakujira (kujira** = whale).

A similar word in vogue today is **burikko,** which is a contraction of "a girl (**ko**) who puts on (**furi** = **buri**) a cute pose." Sometime in the future, if **kamatoto** should ever become obsolete and be replaced by **burikko,** we might have **burikko** who will be asking, "What is **kamatoto?"**

Kamikaze ga fuku

Twice in the thirteenth century—1274 and 1281— Mongol forces attempted to invade Japan, but on both occasions the invading fleet was demolished by a typhoon, and Japan was saved. The people believed that the propitious typhoons were the blessings of god and named them **kamikaze** (divine wind).

The Japanese are not a particularly religious race of people, but in time of distress they do hope for a *deus ex machina* (**kamikaze**) to help them out of the predicament.

When a company cannot get out of difficulties despite all its efforts, it begins to hope for a **kamikaze** to blow (**fuku**), such as an unexpected big order, which provides the impetus for explosive growth.

The contemporary use of **kamikaze** as an adjective to describe a reckless or daredevil taxi driver stems from the name given to the suicide corps

whose pilots crash-dived their planes into enemy craft during the closing phase of the Pacific War.
See also Tanabota.

Kamo

Kamo is a wild duck that migrates to ponds and marshes in Japan every winter. Among them, the kind known as **magamo** is very tasty. The **magamo** is big and always moves around in flocks, making it comparatively easy prey for hunters.

Because of this, a pushover or a sucker is called a **kamo**. If an opponent appears to be weak, people say, "I'll make him a **kamo**": He will be a pushover for me.

The flavor of a **kamo** dish is greatly enhanced when it is cooked with **negi** (green onion). Thus, **kamo ga negi wo shotte kuru** (duck comes carrying **negi**), or shortened as **kamo-negi,** is an expression that means favorable terms are heaped on what is already a good thing.

People who are inexperienced in the ways of the world, such as the sons of wealthy families who have led a sheltered life and housewives, are readily made into **kamo** by (are easy prey for) calculating people. If one has fallen prey to the guile of calculating people, the term to use is **ejiki ni sareta** (fallen prey to).
See also Ippai kū.

Kangaete okimasu

If the Japanese you are negotiating with tells you in English, "I'll think it over" or "I'll give it a thought," don't go away feeling that you might get a favorable answer. Like as not, what the Japanese said was a literal translation of **kangaete okimasu,** and he probably believed that he conveyed to you the nuance contained in the Japanese expression.

When a Japanese hears **kangaete okimasu,** he generally concludes that it is hopeless, because in the unwritten rules of social communiction in Japan, it is a polite way of saying "no." Conversely, if you tell a Japanese "I'll think it over," he might take it that you mean **kangaete okimasu** and that he has been refused.

If both sides were familiar with the difference between **kangaete okimasu** and "I'll think it over," there would be less chance of misunderstanding.

See also Zensho shimasu.

Kangei-kai and Sōbetsu-kai

The frequent holding of a **kangei-kai** (welcoming party) by businessmen as well as by people in other walks of life, is one of the ways in which the Japanese exhibit their "groupism."

When new recruits join a company, a **kangei-kai** is held to welcome them. When a person is assigned to a new department, he is welcomed with a **kangei-kai.** When a staff member returns from an overseas assignment, he also is given a **kangei-kai. Sake** flows at the **kangei-kai,** and the atmosphere is relaxed. The **kangei-kai** plays a very important role in Japanese society, because it helps strengthen the newcomer's (or returnee's) feeling of belonging, enhances group spirit, promotes solidarity, and develops a sense of identity.

The opposite of the welcoming party is the **sōbetsu-kai** (farewell or sendoff party), which usually turns out to be rather emotional. When a newcomer comes to take the place of a departing member, it is customary to combine the two parties into a single **kansōgei-kai**.

See also Bōnen-kai.

Kanko-dori ga naku

Kanko-dori is the name of the Japanese cuckoo, a bird that comes to Japan around May every year and migrates to the south in autumn.

When the cuckoo cries (**kanko-dori ga naku**), it creates a lonely and even desolate feeling. When they say in the business world that the cuckoo is crying, it means customers are few and far between. When the plant operating rate falls, machinery becomes idle, and the workers spend their time mowing grass in the factory enclosure, then the cuckoo's cry can be heard. (In Japan, because it is not customary to lay off workers, the company retains idle workers on its payroll even in times of recession.)

The term, however, is used mostly in businesses that cater to individual customers, such as a bar or cabaret. At a bar where not a single customer is seen and hostesses are idly waiting for one to walk in, the cuckoo is crying.

Kao

Kao (face) can be a vital factor in conducting business in any country. The great importance the Japanese attach to it is seen from the many expressions in the language that use **kao.**

First among these is, of course, **kao wo tateru** (to give face or to save face). Extended meanings of this can be ''for your sake'' and ''to prevent one from disgrace or dishonor.'' Because consideration for the other party's honor and reputation is so important in Japanese human relations, this expression is heard all the time. The opposite of giving face is **kao wo tsubusu** (to cause a loss of face).

In doing business, it is an advantage to be a person whose **kao ga hiroi**—a person who has many contacts. A person who has many contacts is constantly doing things to **kao wo tsunagu**—keep up contacts already made. He might do so by casually dropping in at the other person's office from time to time, inviting him to lunch or golf, sending gifts at the midsummer and year-end gift-giving seasons, and never failing to send New Year's greetings.

Having many contacts with ordinary people isn't as useful as knowing persons whose **kao ga kiku.** These are people with influence, those whose word carries a lot of weight.

The Japanese also say **kao wo uru,** whose direct translation, ''to sell face,'' tells you at once that it means ''to sell or advertise oneself.''

The face can also be ''loaned,'' as in the expression **kao wo kasu.** ''Lend me your face'' (**kao wo kase**) would mean ''I want to have a talk with you.''

Many of the expressions that deal with the face are regarded as underworld lingo. **Kao wo uru** and **kao wo kasu,** in particular, have a strong underworld tone.

Kara-oke

Kara is the Japanese word meaning "empty" and **oke** is the first part of the Japanese pronunciation of the English word "orchestra." The Japanese have a special talent for creating synthetic words of this type. Examples: **katsu-don** (**katsu** = cutlet; **donburi** = bowl), which means rice in a bowl topped with pork cutlet; **han-zubon** (**han** = half; **zubon** = **jupon** = pants), which means short pants; **jari-tare** (**jari** = child; **tarento** = talent), which means a child entertainer; **nama-kon** (**nama** = crude, half-done, rare; **konkurīto** = concrete), which means ready-mix cement. The examples are inexhaustible.

Kara-oke is a device for playing an orchestra accompaniment recorded on cassette tape. Bars and **aka-chōchin** everywhere have **kara-oke** for the convenience of customers who are feeling high and want to display their singing talent to an orchestral accompaniment. People who have never met each other before will join in the singing and clink drinking cups together. **Kara-oke** singing is a nuisance to a person who wants to enjoy his drink quietly. However, for the harried corporate worker the **kara-oke** bar is unexcelled as a place to work off steam and to refresh himself after a hard day's work.

See also Aka-chōchin.

Katabō wo katsugu

The literal translation of this would be "to carry (**katsugu**) one end of a pole (**katabō**) on one's shoulder." Its meaning is "to take part in," "to be a partner in." In the old days, people were transported in a palanquin, which had a pole protruding in front and back. One bearer in front and another at the back put their shoulders under the ends of the pole to lift up and move the palanquin.

This expression is used more often than not in describing participation in some unsavory matter. It is not used so often when people pull together for a good cause. Thus, the term carries a critical tone, possibly because unscrupulous palanquin bearers sometimes carried a passenger into a dark corner and robbed him of his valuables.

Another expression that comes from the carrying of the palanquin is **kata wo ireru** (put the shoulder under the pole). This does not have a bad connotation. It is used to mean supporting a **sumō** wrestler or an entertainer such as a singer and helping him to gain popularity.

See also Mikoshi.

Kata-tataki

Kata-tataki is a word dreaded by government employees who are past the age of fifty-five or so. The term simply means "tap on the shoulder," but in the civil service it has an ominous ring. A worker is approached gently by his superior—an actual physical tap on the shoulder may not take place—with a hint that it's about time he retired from the service.

In the civil service, there is no fixed compulsory retirement age. Unless a worker retires of his own will, the government cannot fire him. Thus, there are cases of workers staying on even past seventy. It is for this reason that the **kata-tataki** form is employed when a government department feels that the usefulness of a worker has ended because of his advanced age.

A few people resist, but in general most government employees take the hint, because if they do, they will be promoted one rank and receive a larger retirement allowance and pension.

See also Kibō-taishoku.

Katte-deru

Katte-deru is a colorful expression essentially meaning "to volunteer." But often it conveys a nuance that goes beyond simple volunteering. For instance, it is often used to mean "to undertake a task or challenge which others shun, although one was not asked to do so and although it is not really one's business.

The expression literally means "pay to enter the fray," and it originated as a gambling term. In a card game in which the number of players was limited, a latecomer had to pay money to someone already seated at the table to buy a seat so that he could enter the game. From this, **katte-deru** came to mean "getting into the act voluntarily from the sidelines."

Kayui-tokoro ni te ga todoku

Literally translated, this turns out as "the hand reaches the itchy place." When any part of the body feels itchy, there is no greater feeling than scratching it or having someone else scratch it for you if it is in the small of the back. For aged people whose hand is no longer so flexible as to reach around to the back, a back-scratching stick has been made and is inspiringly called **mago-no-te** (grandchild's hand), because in the old days it was the dutiful grandchild's chore to scratch the grandparent's itchy back.

When, as a guest or as a customer, one's every wish is attended to, it equals the satisfying delight of having one's itchy back scratched. Thus, the expression is used to mean "to be attentive to one's every wish."

This is the posture most demanded of people engaged in the service industry and of those who serve others. If the attentive service showered on a person should miss the itchy point, the effect would be to make that person feel impatient or even irritated. This is called **kakka-sōyō,** which means scratching an itch ineffectively. Thus, **kayui-tokoro ni te ga todoku** implies that one must have precise knowledge of the needs and wishes of the person one wants to serve.

Keiko

The original meaning of this word is "to ponder about old things and learn about them" or "to read and learn from old books." But hardly any present-day Japanese is aware of this original meaning. The first mutation changed the meaning to mean "practice what one learned." Thus **keiko** came to mean practicing **kendō** (fencing) and **jūdō** in a training hall. Today's people use **keiko** to mean practicing swimming, various types of exercises in an athletic gym, and even jazz dancing, the current rage.

Going secretly to learn **kouta** (singing of ditties) to make it one's **kakushi-gei** is also considered as **keiko**. When women use the honorific and say **o-keiko,** the reference is to lessons for acquiring such accomplishments as playing the **koto** (Japanese harp), flower arrangement (**ikebana**), and tea ceremony. Companies with a large female staff provide the girls with company-paid **o-keiko** lessons.

Keiko-goto is the general word meaning learning of traditional artistic accomplishments. The learning of such things as swimming, piano, and ballet is called **ressun,** the Japanese pronunciation of "lesson."

See also Kakushi-gei.

Kekkō desu

You will hear this phrase spoken very often at the dinner table. But watch out. It can mean "This tastes good," or "No thanks, I've had enough," or "That's a good idea. I'll have another helping." Which of these three is meant depends on the situation, the speaker's intonation, and sometimes the linkage with other words.

Because of its three meanings, it lends itself to some good-natured fun. The hostess asks, "Won't you have some more?" The guest answers, "**kekkō desu,**" meaning that he has had enough. The hostess shoots back, "If you think it's **kekkō,** (meaning 'splendid'), you must have some more." But it's not just a dinner table word. In any situation, it can be used in its three meanings of "good, fine, etc.," "I've had enough, I'm satisfied," or "with pleasure."

Kemu ni maku

A literal translation of this expression is sufficient to indicate what it means. Envelop (**maku**) in smoke (**kemu** or **kemuri**). Smoke cuts down visibility. When one is wrapped in smoke, he can't see things correctly and thus becomes bewildered and unsure of things. The expression is different from putting up a smoke screen.

The expression is used to describe an operation in which the other party's unfamiliarity with or ignorance of a matter is taken advantage of. The proponent one-sidedly and skillfully makes an exaggerated but reasonable-sounding presentation, overwhelming the other party into thinking that the proposal being made is right.

After the parties leave the negotiating table, the smoke, too, is left behind. So, even if during the negotiations the proponent may have thought that he had successfully carried out his **kemu ni maku** operation, at contract-signing time the other party may come back with cogent and logical arguments to expose his ruse. The moral is that it is better to be sincere at all times in business negotiations.

Ki

Ki is a versatile word whose meanings include spirit, mind, heart, will, intention, feelings, mood, nature, and disposition—the abstract qualities which concern the heart and mind. It can also mean care, precaution, attention, air, atmosphere, flavor, and smell. Expressions given here are those which relate to the first group of meanings.

A very popular expression is **ki wa kokoro** ("ki is heart"), which means that the gesture may be small but it shows sincerity or goodwill or genuine gratitude or desire to help.

If you feel **ki ni kuwanai** about the performance of your subordinate, you think it is unsatisfactory or you are displeased with it. If you feel your boss is a **ki ni kuwanai** person, it means you think he is a disagreeable fellow (see **Hada ni awanai**). The opposite is **ki ni iru**: to like, to find agreeable, to suit one's taste, etc.

When a person "pulls out the **ki**" (**ki wo nuku**), it means he has become unenthusiastic, lukewarm, discouraged, dispirited, careless. When "**ki** does not go into" (**ki ga hairanu**) any endeavor or undertaking, it means one cannot become enthusiastic about it.

Ki can also be rubbed or massaged—**ki wo momu**. In this case, a person is worried or anxious about something and becomes nervous and fidgety. **Ki wo momaseru** is to keep a person in suspense or on tenterhooks.

Ki wo hiku (draw the **ki**) is to sound out the intentions of the other party.

Kinori usu (the **ki** is thin), which means lackluster, lethargic, stagnant, or unenthusiastic, can be used to describe the performance of the stock market.

Kibō-taishoku

Under Japan's lifetime employment system, all corporations have a compulsory retirement age, which at present generally ranges between 55 and 60. The retiring employee automatically receives a retirement allowance calculated according to a ratio indexed to his length of service and basic salary. In the event an employee resigns for personal reasons before his automatic retirement age, the allowance will be reduced considerably below the standard.

When the big jump in oil prices reduced corporate earnings, many companies adopted the policy of "weight-reducing" to cut down overhead. Instead of dismissing, say, one hundred employees outright, the company asked for voluntary resignations of one hundred employees, offering as an inducement allowances considerably more than the standard sum. Employees who took advantage of this offer were treated as **kibō-taishoku,** literally, leaving the company of their own wish, but different from resigning for personal reasons, or **jiko-taishoku.**

See also Jihyō, Kata-tataki.

Kimon

The ancient Japanese believed that the devil (**ki** or **oni**) came from the northeast. Thus, the northeast corner was regarded as unlucky, and it was taboo to situate the front door or gate (**mon**) in the northeast corner, because it would make it easier for the devil to bring in all sorts of misfortune. It was also taboo to situate the kitchen and the washroom in the northeast corner. The southwest corner is known as the **ura** (rear) **kimon** and is also an unlucky direction. This taboo restricted the options for house designers and taxed the planning ability of carpenters.

This led to the use of the word **kimon** as a sort of code to refer to a person one finds difficult to negotiate or to deal with or to matters in which one is inept. Thus, one's boss might say to his subordinate, "The president of that company is my **kimon,** so will you go and talk to him?" Or "My son's **kimon** in school is mathematics."

The devil is regarded as the whip-driver of Hell and in Japanese pictures it is depicted with horns and wearing short pants made of tiger skin.

Kogai

Originally **kogai** meant a pet, like a dog or cat, which one brought up from a puppy or a kitten, or the act of doing so.

The word later came to be used to refer to a person who apprenticed himself as a child to work under a merchant or artisan under the old teacher–disciple system. Today, a person who receives the favors and patronage of a superior under whom he has served since joining the company is called the **kogai** of that superior. Such a person would be a devoted and trusted subordinate.

The contrasting word is **tozama.** Originally the opposite of **tozama** was **fudai,** which referred to a hereditary vassal, or successive generations of the same family serving under the same feudal lord's family. This latter word is not used so much in today's business society, because it is rare for successive generations of the same family to work in the same company, and still rarer for father and son to be the subordinates of the same boss.

See also Tozama.

Konjō

A businessman who is described as **konjō ga aru** (possessing **konjō**) is one who has "fighting spirit, will power, determination, tenacity, and guts." He is a person who gets things done even against great odds. Adversity never gets him down. In fact, adversity spurs him on to greater efforts. He is a tough negotiator who never gives up. The opposite is **konjō ga nai.**

To his boss, the **konjō ga aru** subordinate is one who can be trusted to carry out the most difficult assignment without a word of complaint. The boss does not have to keep looking over his shoulder or give him pep talks. **Konjō** therefore is that extra element, aside from expertise or experience, which gives an added value to a businessman.

Kōsai-hi

In general, **kōsai-hi** is money spent for maintaining social contacts or entertaining friends. In the business world it is the entertainment expense account.

Although business entertainment is a common practice in all parts of the world, it probably plays a bigger role in Japan than in other countries. This is because human relations are all-important in Japanese society, and **sake** lubricates those relations better than anything else.

It is said that the majority of expensive bars and nightclubs in Tokyo would close overnight if the expense account system were abolished, because they are patronized almost wholly by people with fat expense accounts. Under today's depressed business conditions, more and more business entertainment is taking the form of a lunch instead of expensive wining and dining at night.

See also Shayō-zoku.

Koshi

As the pivotal part of the body, the **koshi** (waist, hip, loin) appears in many expressions that describe things as being one way or the other.

For instance, we say **koshi ga hikui** (low) or **takai** (high). Low waist means humble, modest, unassuming, and polite; conversely, high waist means proud, haughty.

A person whose **koshi ga karui** (light) is one who is quick to act, nimble, or willing to work. Conversely, the person whose waist is **omoi** (heavy) is one who is slow to act or unwilling to work, or who dilly-dallies. It is not advisable to say **koshi ga karui** of a woman, because it can be taken to mean she flits from one man to another.

Koshi wo ageru is to raise the waist, which not

only means that a person gets up physically from a sitting position but also described a person who has just been watching the situation and has now decided to take action (see **Mikoshi**).

Koshi wo sueru is to let the waist settle down, which means settling down to a steady course of action or undertaking something seriously or with determination.

To do something with **oyobi-goshi** is to do it in an unsteady position, with bent back or leaning over. Thus, it is used to describe a person whose heart is not in his work.

Koshi-kudake is a person whose "waist breaks down," a weak-kneed person. Coming from a **sumō** (Japanese wrestling) term meaning breaking down in the middle of a bout, it usually describes a person who falls apart at a crucial moment in, say, business negotiations.

When some event causes a person's "hip to go out of joint" (**koshi ga nukeru**), he is overwhelmed by the magnitude of the occasion or paralyzed with fear.

Koshikake

By itself **koshikake** merely means a chair or a place to sit. But it is a word popularly used in Japanese companies in quite a different context.

How would you interpret it if you should hear a Japanese say, "I am in this company only as a **koshikake**"? Certainly, he couldn't mean that he is a chair. Or "The vice president's post is a **koshikake** for Mr. Tanaka"? Or "Girl university graduates regard jobs in big corporations only as a **koshi-kake**"? Puzzling? Not if you substitute for **koshikake** in each question the concepts "a temporary position while looking for something better," "a stepping-stone to a higher post," and "a place to fill time before getting married."

In other words, **koshikake** is used to describe a post regarded not as permanent but as a transit point.

Kubi

Japanese in responsible positions are fond of the expression **kubi wo kakete,** meaning "stake my neck," with the neck (**kubi**) standing for position, honor, reputation, or even life. It is an expression of confidence and determination in undertaking some big task.

Of course, in a Japanese corporation it is pretty safe to "stake one's neck," because under the life-time employment system it is rare that one's **kubi ga tobu** (to be fired). This is not to say that companies never carry out **kubi-kiri** (personnel reduction), because extreme business conditions sometimes do make it necessary to scale down a company's operations in order to survive.

When a company, or an individual for that matter, finds itself up to its neck in debt (**kubi ga mawaranai,** or "cannot turn the neck"), it has to **kubi wo hineru** (wring the neck = rack the brain, think hard) to devise ways to get out of its straitened circumstances.

A euphemistic Japanese expression which uses the word **kubi** is **mawata de kubi wo shimeru.** The latter part of this expression translates as "strangle the neck." **Mawata** is delicate silk floss that is pleasant to the skin. Strangling a person with floss means using a gentle or indirect way to throttle a person gradually. It is used to describe an operation for easing a person out by gradually making it impossible for him to stay.

See also Hara (tsume-bara).

Kugi wo sasu

An alternate expression is **kugi wo utsu, sasu** and **utsu** being synonymous. When making wooden furniture, if mortise and tenon joints are glued together, it should be enough.

However, if a nail **(kugi)** is driven in **(sasu, utsu),** it makes doubly sure that the joint will be fast.

Stemming from this, **kugi wo sasu** has come to be used to mean an act of confirmation to make sure. A synonym is **dame wo osu.** This is the operation in the game of **go** to confirm the result at the end of a match.

Kugi wo sasu is also the act of making sure that roof tiles and sashes would not be blown away in a typhoon. Thus, the expression is also used to mean giving a warning so that the other party would not veer in an undesirable direction.

When the wife "drives in the nail" by saying, "You promised to take the children to the amusement park tomorrow morning, so please come home early today," the husband will be unable to enjoy **hashigo-zake,** even though the next day may be a holiday.

See also Hashigo, Dame-oshi.

Kuromaku

The first part of the ideogram for **kuromaku** is written with the Chinese character for "black," and the latter part with the character for "curtain." In the old days, it used to be the backdrop behind a stage. Today, when a person is called a **kuromaku,** it means he is an influential man behind the scenes, the wire-puller who is hidden from public view or who doesn't hold an official post.

Such characters abound in every society, mostly in politics and government. Sometimes it has a sinister connotation. In business, they are not found in individual corporations, but there might be a **kuromaku** who is influential in a particular industry as a whole.

See also Ōgosho.

Ma

The basic meaning of **ma** is space, interval, time. Branching out from these are the meanings of chance, luck, occasion.

Ma wo motasu is "to fill in time" under special circumstances. For instance, people are gathered at a business meeting or a party at which a certain thing is planned to take place. But before the time for it comes, an unexpected time gap occurs. To keep people entertained or occupied so that interest does not flag is **ma wo motasu**.

Ma wo ireru is literally "put in time," but not in the English sense of "serve." Here **ma** means an intentional pause or interval of time before taking action because certain considerations make such a pause necessary or desirable or strategically effective.

Ma ga warui is "**ma** is bad," but the reference is not to time but to situation. It means embarrassing and sometimes even unlucky.

Ma ga nukeru is "**ma** slips out," meaning "not in tune with things" or "out of place." "**Ma**" is something that is necessary at a given time or on a given occasion. If that something should be out of line or out of tune with respect to time or quality or character, it becomes useless or **ma-nuke** (**ma** is missing). Thus, a **ma-nuke** person is stupid, silly, slow-witted, dumb. When you are exasperated with a person's bungling and want to shout at him that he is an idiot, this is the word to use.

Madogiwa-zoku

Madogiwa is "beside the window" and **zoku** is "tribe." In almost every big Japanese business corporation you will find the "window-side tribe." They are people of the middle-echelon manager class who usually have the title of manager or submanager but no functions and duties.

Although in their younger days they played a

very active part in the company's business, their climb up the promotion ladder has stopped. Under the seniority system, in order to make way for younger people, they have been removed from active duty. Under the lifetime employment system, however, they cannot be dismissed. And, in view of their rank, they are given desks in the best place in the office—beside the window—where they sit waiting for their retirement age to come. Thus, **madogiwa-zoku** is a word with a pathetic ring.

Mae-daoshi

When a streetcar or a car brakes suddenly, the passengers fall forward. This falling forward is called **mae-daoshi.** The term was adopted in government finance to mean front-loading of public works expenditure for the purpose of stimulating the economy. When, for instance, the central or local government disburses in the second quarter the public works appropriations budgeted for the third quarter, it is called **mae-daoshi** (front-loading).

The word is also used in business corporations, but with a different meaning. In their case, it is the advancing of the schedule for a project. Because the schedules for all operations are tied together, it calls for greater efforts all around.

In the case of government budgets, the measure that is the reverse of front-loading would be the deferring of disbursements. For business corporations, there is no such thing as deferring or putting back the schedule for the achievement of a project.

When such a thing happens it simply becomes failure to achieve.

Maemukini

The word itself simply means "in the forward (**mae**) direction (**muki**)" and can be understood to mean "positively." However, when it is used in conversation, particularly negotiations, it conveys a meaning with a different nuance.

Kangaete okimasu (I'll give it a thought) is the roundabout Japanese way of saying "no" and that one cannot expect any result from **zensho shimasu** (I shall do my best to respond to your wishes).

If you are told **maemukini kangaete okimasu,** you can feel relieved, because it does not mean "no." It gives you a very slight hope—**myaku ga aru** (pulse is still beating).

If the other party says **maemukini zensho shimasu,** you can cling to the hope that his intention is not to disregard your proposition completely.

In both cases, big expectations should not be entertained. They just mean "it is not a completely final no." The probability, however, is that nothing concrete will come of it.

See also Myaku, Kangaete okimasu, Zensho shimasu.

Mai hōmu

The Japanese businessman is generally thought of as an eager-beaver employee racing on the promotional track in the company. He drudges all day long, sacrificing the time that businessmen in other countries use to spend with their family. He does not use up the annual holidays to which he is entitled, because he thinks he is so indispensable in the company's day-to-day operation that he must be at the office all the time.

A generation ago, the above description applied to almost all Japanese. But not everybody is a workaholic these days. More and more businessmen of the younger generation are having second thoughts about the traditional values. They value family life as much as or more than business career. Their numbers have increased so much that a word has been coined for such people: **Mai-hōmu-shugi-sha** (my-home-ist).

Mā-mā

"How's your business?" "**Mā-mā desu.**" (Not so bad, not so good.) "How did you like the new French restaurant?" "Did you enjoy the movie last night?" The answer can be "**mā-mā,**" meaning "so-so." The expression usually implies lukewarm approval rather than disapproval. Sometimes it is purely noncommittal, masking a lack of opinion.

Sometimes it is used in an obviously positive context. "My business is **mā-mā**" could actually mean "quite good," but the speaker is trying to be modest.

When your Japanese friends ask for your impressions about Japan, **mā-mā** is not recommended as an answer, because you will be taking the risk of implying that you haven't really enjoyed your experience in Japan.

Meishi

The calling (business) card is a must in social and particularly business contacts in Japan. When one meets somebody for the first time, the **meishi** is exchanged instead of shaking hands as in the West. Any businessman who cannot produce a **meishi** has one strike against him. Businessmen keep a file of the cards they collect, and this is invaluable when the time comes to send out Christmas or New Year greeting cards.

Many Japanese businessmen have bilingual **meishi** with name, position, company name, address, and phone number in Japanese on one side and in English on the other. If foreign businessmen visiting Japan want to be remembered, they should have their **meishi** printed in the same manner. In major hotel arcades, there is usually a shop that offers twenty-four-hour printing of **meishi.**

Mikoshi

Mikoshi is the portable **shinto** shrine which a group of young men in **happi** coats carry (**katsugu**) around the local parish on their shoulders during the annual festival while shouting "Wasshoi! Wasshoi!" It's a lively show which attracts big crowds. The expression **mikoshi wo katsugu** is used when people form a group to support or promote someone, such as a candidate in an election.

A commonly used expression in which the word appears is **mikoshi wo ageru** which means "get up from one's seat" or "take one's leave" after staying a bit too long. When one sits down for a long talk, it is **mikoshi wo suete hanashikomu,** which can also mean he is overstaying his welcome.

See also Koshi (wo ageru/sueru).

Miso

Miso is paste made by fermenting salted soybeans. Like soy sauce, it is a flavoring indispensable in Japanese cuisine. Because it is so close to the life of the people, it is used figuratively in many Japanese expressions.

Because **miso** is a flavoring that makes the difference in cooking dishes, it is used in figures of speech to mean a "good or advantageous point." For instance, "The **miso** of this business is that we can avail ourselves of the distribution network of our tie-in partner."

In the old days, each family made its own **miso** at home. From this practice, the expression **temaemiso** (**miso** of one's own making) was born. This is used to describe the act of self-praise—boasting about one's own performance or ability.

On the one hand, **miso wo tsukeru** (apply **miso**) and **miso ga tsuku** (tainted with **miso**) are expressions meaning to make a blunder that blemishes one's otherwise excellent record. This meaning comes from the fact that **miso** has a dirty appearance—like reddish brown mud. The blunder so described is not a fatal one; it only slightly spoils an otherwise good reputation.

See also Chonbo.

Miya-zukae

Miya refers to the imperial court or the home of nobles. **Miya-zukae** originally meant "to serve in a **miya**," but today it is used to mean service in the government or a business corporation.

Whether in the case of the original **miya-zukae** or his present-day counterpart, anyone serving under another person has to perform work he may not like and has to endure a lot of things. Therefore, the expression contains the rather forlorn feeling of the salaried worker: "All bosses make unreasonable demands, but we have to humor him. We have to endure unpleasant things because we are working for a living."

Employed workers since the feudal days have expressed this feeling by quoting a famous line from Kabuki drama: "**Sumajiki mono wa miya-zukae**" = "The life of a government official is really an unenvious one," which can be paraphrased to mean "one must put up with all kinds of humiliation as long as one is in the service of another."

Because of this nuance, when you are introducing yourself as a company employee, you should never say "I am a **miya-zukae**."

Mizu

Mizu is water, but when you hear the word **mizu-shōbai** (water business) do not jump to the conclusion that it is the business of selling water. The word is used to describe a business whose earnings are greatly dependent on its popularity with customers. Specifically it means establishments like nightclubs, restaurants, and theaters.

Figurative expressions using **mizu** are mostly easy to understand. **Mizu wo sasu** (to pour water) can readily be imagined as meaning "to pour cold water on" or "to put a damper on." The expression describes the act of a person who says or does a thing to put a brake on or foul up something that is proceeding smoothly. It is also used to mean "discourage a person" from carrying on with what he has been doing. Another sense in which the expression is used is "to alienate one person from another."

Mizu-kake-ron (a water-dousing argument) is an argument or discussion that reaches no conclusion. It's like the argument over which came first, the chicken or the egg. After a confrontation, the Japanese usually **mizu ni nagasu** (flush the water) which means "wash out the past" or "let bygones be bygones."

An often-used saying is **gaden-insui,** which is literally "to draw water into (one's) paddy field." It describes the act of using given facts to one's own advantage in a debate or taking advantage of something to justify one's standpoint.

Mizuhiki torihiki means engineering a transaction by first taking a small loss in order to obtain a bigger profit later.

Yobi-mizu is "calling water" = priming water. It means something that serves as a lead-in to something else.

Mōretsu

This word was used during Japan's high growth decade of the 1960s to describe the corporate employee who had only work on his mind. When World War II ended, Japan was in shambles, and the people had to start from zero in order to rebuild the country. The only way they could do it was to work in a **mōretsu** (furious) way. Corporate employees of those days left home early in the morning and did not return until late at night. Day after day, they worked long hours of overtime and hardly took any vacations. They worked themselves to the bone in order to bring bigger profits to the company. Partly in good-natured fun, the mass media applauded such dedicated employees as **mōretsu shain.**

The **mōretsu shain** were the yeomen behind the scenes who helped Japan to achieve a GNP second in the world. The outside world's word for such hard-working Japanese was "workaholics." Today, with Japan having become affluent, it is no longer fashionable to be **mōretsu.**

However, this does not mean that dedication to the company has waned. It's just that they don't have to work such long hours any more, because the economy's foundation has been built, and bigger returns can be achieved with less effort.

Myaku

This word means "vein," and it indicates the connection between things: **jin-myaku** (personal connections), **san-myaku** (mountain range), **ketsu-myaku** (blood vessel). It also means the pulse beat.

Myaku ga aru (pulse exists) means that there is still life and is used to indicate that even in a very dismal situation hope is still not dead. It is used in such ways as, ''Judging from this morning's telex message this deal still has **myaku**,'' and ''The president did not show much interest in the project, but because the managing director, who has a lot of power, is favorably inclined, the project still has **myaku**.''

It is said that in feudal days, physicians measured the shogun's pulse from an adjoining room with the help of a string tied around the shogun's wrist. True or not, it must be very difficult to conduct a diagnosis by such a method. Today, businessmen **myaku wo miru** (take the pulse) of a project or transaction by depending on small bits of information (= string).

Used in the same meaning is **dashin suru** (sound out), which comes from the way the doctor taps on the patient's breast to diagnose him.

See also Jin-myaku.

Naishoku

In feudal days, **naishoku** meant the sideline of a **samurai** or the work done by **rōnin**. Today, it generally means the manual piecework a housewife does at home. The number of housewives who work outside the home in part-time jobs or as cosmetics and life insurance saleswomen has increased recently, but this type of work is not called **naishoku**. Such work is known as **arubaito**. When a housewife holds down a permanent job, it is known as either **tomo-bataraki** (working together) or **tomo-kasegi** (earning together), assuming of course that her husband is working too. **Naishoku,** it seems, is the word reserved for work done at home for money.

When a corporate employee takes home work from the office, he might say jokingly, ''I am going to do **naishoku** tonight,'' although he will not receive payment for it. These days, some people use their weekends to write a novel at home, which falls under **naishoku**. But if, say, carpentering is your hobby, you would not describe it as doing **naishoku**. You are a Sunday carpenter or a Sunday artist, as the case may be.

See also Arubaito.

Nakatta-koto ni suru

This means to start afresh—to revert to the situation before an event.

When a sudden turn of events makes it impossible to fulfill a previously made commitment, a person **naki wo irete** and gets the other party to agree that there was no such commitment. This is **nakatta-koto ni suru.** In the case of a business commitment made by signing a contract, it is not possible to **nakatta-koto ni suru,** but in personal relations it happens quite often, with or without the payment of a penalty.

In either case, the side that benefits from **nakatta-koto ni suru** incurs a **giri** (obligation) vis-à-vis the other party. At some time in the future he would have to pay back the debt. Although the two sides agree to forget that a promise existed, the side that benefits from this arrangement must never forget that he is now under a new obligation.

Even if a contract has a *force majeure* clause that makes it **nakatta-koto,** in the case of a contract between Japanese parties the slate is not necessarily wiped clean. **Giri** remains on one side or the other. *See also* Giri, Naki.

Nakazu tobazu

King Chuang (end of seventh century B.C.) of Ch'u in China's age of the Warring States immersed himself in play and pleasure and neglected state affairs. Anyone who criticized his behavior was punished by death. One day, a retainer gave the king a riddle: "A bird is perched on top of a hill for three years without flying or without letting out a single cry. What is the name of this bird?" The king replied: "If a bird does not cry (**nakazu**) and not fly (**tobazu**) for three years, when it does fly it will rise to heaven and when it does cry it will astonish people. I understand what you mean." After that, King Chuang mended his ways, put his heart into governing the country, and became known in history as one of the five most able kings of the Warring States of China.

The expression is used in Japan today to describe a person of whom much is expected but who fails to accomplish anything. For instance, "Although he scored the best mark in the company entrance examination, after entering the company, he is **nakazu tobazu.**"

Although the Chinese king eventually did cry and fly, the expression as used in Japan today carries the nuance that the person so described is not likely to improve in the future and that appearances were deceitful in his case.

Naki

This means "cry" or "weep." Although it is regarded in the world of men as shameful to be caught crying, there are many semantic ways in which Japanese men cry.

Naki-neiri, literally, is "sleep crying." A deal on the point of being concluded is unexpectedly snatched away by a rival. One's cherished proposal is squelched or shelved because of intervention from the manager of a different department. In such a case, one cannot unburden his chagrin to anybody, so he cries on his pillow, figuratively.

Naki wo miru: A project that was going smoothly suddenly flounders without any hope of recovery. In such a situation, one cannot help but cry. So he sees (**miru**) his own crying face.

Naki-tsura ni hachi is the expression to use when one misfortune comes on top of another. It is as if one is stung in the face (**tsura**) by a bee (**hachi**) when he is already crying over an earlier misfortune or failure.

Naki wo ireru is the plea "please give me another chance."

Naki-dokoro, literally "crying place," means a person's weakness, weak point, or Achilles' heel.

See also Nakatta-koto ni suru, Nigiri-tsubushi.

Naniwa-bushi

This is the name of a popular performing art. It was perfected to its present form in the late nineteenth century in Osaka (whose old name was Naniwa) from a street minstrel act, and since then spread widely throughout the country.

The theme of **naniwa-bushi** (**bushi** = tune, melody) is mostly the tragic separation of mother and child, or the doings of the **yakuza** (underworld characters). Although the **yakuza** were lawless people, their exploits were extolled because they put corrupt government officials in their place. The **yakuza,** moreover, were reputed to place a high value on **giri** and **jingi.**

Thus, "That man is **naniwa-bushi**" has come to mean that he possesses a strong sense of justice, has a sympathetic heart, and acts with decorum. However, it is not all praise, because the word includes the nuance "somewhat thoughtless, lacking in discretion, and apt to be influenced by sentiment." "What he says is **naniwa-bushi**" means "He does not use reason to persuade but appeals only to the emotion."

Although the Japanese are slightly contemptuous of the **naniwa-bushi** approach, they use it as a very important means of promoting human relations.

See also Giri, Jingi.

Nawabari

When entering a feudal castle, one had to pass through the outer gate into a maze of paths and passages, going through many gates. Because ropes (**nawa**) were strung to show the way, **nawa-bari** came to mean the ground plan.

Ropes were also strung to mark off the construction area for which each contractor was responsible. Thus, "This is my **nawabari**" meant "I am responsible for the construction in this place." This turned into "I won't allow anybody to touch this place" and then was extended to mean "This is my sphere of influence."

Today, the expression is used in the last of these meanings. The Monroe Doctrine is a **nawabari** declaration. The territorial assignment of the police is also called **nawabari,** but in this case it has the tone of underworld slang.

Salaried workers use the term when they are making the rounds of drinking establishments at night in the practice known as **hashigo.** When one of them says, "This is my **nawabari,** so leave everything to me," it means that the place is his favorite haunt and that he will take care of the bill. The others can relax and drink without worrying about paying for what they consume.

See also Hashigo.

Negai, Todoke

Negai, meaning request, and **todoke,** meaning report, are forms of paper work that keep the administrative machinery in large Japanese companies flowing smoothly.

Prescribed **negai** and **todoke** forms have to be filled in for routine matters such as requests for leave (annual, sick, maternity, etc.), office supplies, and various payments, as well as reports on change of employee's address, family composition (births, deaths, etc.), minor changes in the work system, and so on.

The **negai** and **todoke** systems also are used in

submitting requests and reports or notification to government offices, concerning both business and private matters. The paper work sometimes may seem troublesome, but it is considered essential to administrative efficiency.

See also Jihyō.

Nemawashi

Literally, **nemawashi** means "to dig around the root of a tree to prepare it for transplanting." Adopted from this, the word refers to the groundwork to enlist support or to secure informal consent from the people concerned prior to a formal decision.

Japanese society operates on group decision or consensus, and **nemawashi** is an indispensable process in achieving consensus. It also avoids open confrontation. In the United States, there is a similar process known as preselling, but a decision may be taken regardless of whether or not everyone concerned is in agreement.

In Japan, a proposal will be revised in the process of **nemawashi** until it is molded into a form acceptable to all. So much time is spent in **nemawashi** that foreign businessmen often become exasperated waiting for a Japanese company to make a decision.

See also Ringi.

Nenkō joretsu

Nenkō means long, continued service. One of the characteristics of Japanese management is the determination of order (**joretsu** = rank) in the company on the basis of the length of service. Wages (**chingin**) are determined according to the **nenkō-joretsu chingin** system. Also, the length of service—rather than ability—is the main criterion for making promotions. In each company, it is an unwritten rule that an employee becomes a subsection chief a fixed number of years after joining the company straight from university and a section manager after another fixed number of years. Of course, when the length of service is the same among a number of candidates for promotion, other factors, such as education and performance, would enter into the decision.

Young men of ability who see an older but incompetent man in a higher post and receiving higher pay often complain about the **nenkō-joretsu** system.

With the economy now in a low-growth era, companies are unable to increase their work force and have on their payroll a greater proportion of middle-aged and older employees. This is making it difficult for them to maintain the **nenkō-joretsu** system.

Newaza-shi

A person skilled in behind-the-scenes negotiations is known as a **newaza-shi.** It derives from the **jūdō** term **newaza,** an offensive technique used by a contestant lying on the mat.

As can be imagined, with his bag of tricks, the **newaza-shi** often engineers an unexpected reversal that completely changes the complexion of things. At other times, with his clandestine maneuverings, he makes possible things that seemed impossible for those operating in the limelight. If a man is known as a **newaza-shi,** he can be relied upon to spring a surprise.

Niban-senji

One of the methods used in Chinese herb medicine is to boil herbs for long hours to extract the essence and to drink the liquid so produced. The essence that remains in the boiled herbs is so little that a second (**niban**) boiling (**senji**) of the same leaves is useless. It would be almost like a second brew of tea.

Niban-senji is thus an expression with a critical tone and means that when the same thing is repeated its effectiveness diminishes greatly. It is used to reprove imitation in such a way as, ''The new magazine X is just a **niban-senji** (copy) of Y, which was such a big hit.''

Of course, there are cases where a company has come out with a **niban-senji** product after seeing another's success and is able to seize the market because of its superior marketing power. This manner of doing business is called **niban-te shōhō** (way of marketing/merchandizing). Those who adopt this method believe that **yanagi no shita ni dojō wa nihiki iru** = there are two loaches (a kind of mudfish) under the same willow tree.

See also Yanagi no shita.

Nigiri-tsubushi

Loosely translated, this becomes "crushing in the hand." A proposal is submitted to the boss. The boss pays hardly any attention to it, let alone pass judgment on it. He does not even refer it to other subordinates or discuss it with his colleagues. He just ignores it. This treatment is called **nigiri-tsubushi.**

The meaning is similar to **tana-age** (to put on the shelf). However, if circumstances should change, there is a possibility that a shelved proposal will be brought down from the shelf for reconsideration. On the other hand, if a proposal has been **nigiri-tsubusareta,** it is dead. If a subordinate does not get any reaction for a long time from his boss on his proposal, he resigns himself to the fact it has been crushed for good.

A corporate employee with a lot of mettle might take his **nigiri-tsubusareta** proposal directly to the managing director or the president. This is called **jikiso** (direct appeal). Therefore, the irresolute manager who is unable to give a clear yes or no to a proposal is taking the risk of having his indecisiveness exposed through his subordinate's **jikiso** to a higher level. However, it takes a great deal of courage and good judgment of the situation for deciding on **jikiso.**

Nippachi

In a strict sense, **nippachi** is not a word, because it is composed of two figures—2 and 8. The figures stand for the second month and the eighth month of the year, or February and August.

Meteorologically, these are the coldest and the hottest months of the year in Japan. But the word has nothing to do with the weather. It is a business term and refers to the fact that February and August are traditionally the months when business is slack in Japan.

"How's business?" you ask, and if it happens to be either February or August, the answer more often than not is "Well, you know, it's **nippachi**." It's so commonly accepted that **nippachi** is bad for business that it is quite often used as an acceptable excuse by people who want to put off a transaction or to delay paying their bills.

See also Kaki-ire-doki.

Noren

In the old days, **noren,** a kind of cloth curtain (cotton or sometimes rope woven with hemp), was hung under the eaves of a house to ward off the sun and to serve as a blind. In the Edo Period (seventeenth–nineteenth centuries), merchants dyed their shop name on the **noren** and hung it under the eaves as a signboard.

From this, the word began to be used to mean a store's reputation and its business rights. Although it may appear that Japan does not have the custom of concluding contracts, merchants made a promise saying "I stake my **noren** on ____." This was like entering into a contract by giving as security his entire personality and his entire reputation. Anyone who behaved in a way to "sully his **noren**" was treated as an incompetent. The **noren** was truly the merchant's face. It is similar to regimental colors. Today, a company's credit and social reputation can be considered its **noren.**

In the old days, it was the practice to "divide the **noren**" (**noren-wake**), which meant giving a clerk with long service a **noren** with the same mark and same name as the master's store to open a separate shop. At times the master gave the clerk financial aid and even some of his own customers. This is somewhat similar to the relationship between the modern franchiser and franchisee.

See also Aka chōchin.

Nukegake

This refers to the act of a warrior who secretly slips out of camp just before the engagement of two armies and carries out a one-man attack on the enemy camp. Because it is a surprise raid, it may turn out to be an initial success. However, the act disrupts the army's discipline and control. If the **nukegake** warrior is defeated, it might provide the enemy with impetus and cause a disastrous defeat to his side.

Thus, army commanders strictly prohibited **nukegake.** However, it was hard to eliminate the **nukegake** of those warriors who sought personal glory.

In today's business society, the word is used in reference to a person who disregards the decisions of his organization or the division of roles and maneuvers secretly alone to score a success before anyone is aware of what he is doing. Glory-seeking human nature is the same today as in the old days. Even if the result is good and praise is heaped on the maverick by his boss, his colleagues will treat him coldly.

In Japanese society where things are done collectively, anyone trying to do a smart thing by himself will often find that in the long run he will be a loser.

Nuruma-yu

The Japanese are famous for their love of the bath— and also for the fact that they prefer a very hot bath (42–45 degrees centigrade). Taking a fast dip in a hot bath is called **karasu no gyōzui** (ablution of a crow). In winter, water of about 36 degrees is comfortable for soaking. However, at this temperature one's body does not warm up, and one would not be able to step out into the open air.

A person who is in a position where there is no stimulus, whose situation is neither good nor bad, and who has no urge to change jobs to open up a new frontier for himself because he likes his current peaceful, quiet situation is said to be soaking in **nuruma-yu** (lukewarm bath).

Datsu-sara (quitting a salaried job and starting one's own small business), which at one time was almost a fad, and going into a venture business are courageous acts of jumping out into the cold outside world, because one is not satisfied with a **nuruma-yu** situation.

Salaried employees of big corporations are apt to

rest back in the comfort of **nuruma-yu,** but if every employee should get into such a state, the company will lose its vigor.

Ōbune ni noru

One doesn't have to be a sailor to know that navigating on rough seas is safer and more comfortable on a big ship (**ōbune**) than in a small boat. Thus, the greenhorn businessman would feel as if he were riding (**noru**) on a big ship when he is assigned to a project under the charge of a veteran reputed for his ability.

When somebody can rest at ease in the knowledge that things will go well because the business in which he is involved is in the hands of a capable person, or because he is one cog in a large, smoothly running machine, he feels that he is on an **ōbune.**

Thus the term can be used to mean "to just tag along and don't worry about anything."

Ōburoshiki

The **furoshiki** is a square cloth, normally about 2 feet on each side, which is used to wrap and carry almost anything. When the word is prefixed with **ō,** meaning "big" (4 feet square), the **f** changes to **b.** The word derives from the custom of old days when the people used cloth to wrap their clothing when they undressed to take a bath (**furo**). After the bath they spread out (**shiki**) the cloth, stood on it, and dressed.

In the old days, traveling salesmen bundled up their goods in **ōburoshiki** almost as big as themselves and carried them on their shoulders from village to village. When people commented on the huge load they carried on their shoulders, some of them probably boasted that they could carry even bigger **ōburoshiki**. Thus, when an overconfident person talks big, people say he spreads out (**hirogeru**) an **ōburoshiki**.

Another expression for "talking big" is **hora wo fuku**. This derived from the conch horn (**hora**), which priests who were undergoing ascetic training deep in the mountains used to contact each other.

See also Charan-poran.

Ocha

In the old days, the drinking of green tea was a privilege that only nobles and priests enjoyed. But when it spread to the masses and tea became an indispensable part of Japanese life, expressions using the word **cha** (tea; prefix **o** is an honorific) began to proliferate. Quite naturally, many such expressions were related to breaks from work, to rest and relax.

Cha ni suru (literally, make into tea) means to ridicule what another person says, to dodge a question, or to disregard an issue by steering the conversation away from the subject. This may have come from the practice of serving tea to persons engaged in a task by saying, **ocha desu yo** (it's time for tea). If a person is concentrating his whole energy on the task at that moment, this becomes an unwelcome interruption. Similar expressions include **cha wo ireru** = hinder, obstruct; **chakasu** = tease, make fun of; and **cha wo yū** = to jest.

Ocha wo nigosu is to make ordinary hot water look like tea (**nigosu** = make cloudy or turbid). From this, the expression is used to mean "gloss over a situation in any old way" or "make things look right only on the surface."

Ocha-no-ko = an easy task; same as **asameshi-mae.**

See also Asameshi-mae, Cha-bōzu, Charan-poran.

Ocha wo nomu

Probably no other people **ocha wo nomu** so frequently during office hours as do the Japanese. Literally translated, it means "drink (**nomu**) tea (**ocha**)," but the expression is used also to cover coffee.

The first thing company workers do when they arrive at the office in the morning is to drink green tea. Tea is again served at midmorning and midafternoon. As soon as a visitor to the office is seated, he is served green tea. Tea is served also at business meetings.

Very frequently, co-workers go out during office hours to a neighboring coffee shop to **ocha wo nomu**. The purpose usually is a tête-à-tête. So, when a person asks a fellow worker, "**Ocha wo nomi-masenka?**" ("How about a cup of tea?"), he is saying, "Let's just the two of us have a chat."

And the chat usually is about personnel matters. Very often, drinking tea together serves as an important way of exchanging information.

Business discussions with clients, too, are also frequently held over **ocha** in a coffee shop.

Odawara-hyōjō

Odawara-hyōjō is something the contemporary world has come to expect of international conferences dealing with controversial political and economic problems. Way back in 1590, when the forces of the warlord Toyotomi Hideyoshi attacked Odawara Castle, the stronghold of Hōjō Ujinao, a war council was held by the besieged forces to discuss whether to resist to the end or to negotiate for a truce. The discussions went on and on without reaching a decision. Since that time, **Odawara-hyōjō** has become a synonym for fruitless debate, inconclusive conferences, and generally endless talk resulting in nothing.

Ōgosho, Insei

Originally, **ōgosho** meant the residence of a retired **shōgun** (feudal military governor) and **insei** the system under which a retired emperor continued to rule. Today, the former term is used mostly to mean the most prominent and influential figure, "the grand old man" in a certain sector of society— industry, letters, medicine, sports, etc. The **ōgosho** is universally recognized as truly a man of great stature. He may be retired or still active.

Insei today refers to a situation in which a person

continues to wield great power in an organization or field from which he has already retired. He is able to do so because his successor is weak and dependent on him or because he built up an especially strong personal power base before he officially retired from his post.

Ohako

Ohako is an art or a skill in which one excels. In other words, it means one's forte or speciality. The reference is to something specific rather than general. For instance, one's **ohako** would not be the general "playing golf" but the specific "putting." Some golfer's **ohako** may be to hit a bunker every time. At a party, participants are often called upon to perform their **ohako,** which may be a song, sleight-of-hand, or some other trick.

The Chinese characters for **ohako** can also be read **jūhachiban,** meaning No. 18. The original expression, which is still used today, is **Kabuki jū-hachiban,** meaning the eighteen best plays in the repertoire of the Ichikawa family of Kabuki actors. How did the characters for 18 come to be read **ohako,** which literally means "honorable box"? One theory is that the Ichikawa family carefully kept the manuals on how to act the eighteen plays in a box (**hako**).

See also Kakushi-gei.

Oisogashii desuka?

This translates literally as "Are you busy?" If a Japanese should say these words in greeting, you should not react angrily with, "It's none of your business." It is used merely as a greeting, just like "**Dochira-e?**" and the asker does not expect a concrete answer.

Another way of greeting with a question is "**Mō-karimakka?**" = Are you making a profit? Because this smacks of mercantilism, it is not so generally used.

In Japan, where being busy is a virtue, it is the businessman's protocol to greet their acquaintances with an "**Oisogashii desuka?**" The standard noncommittal response is **mā-mā desu** (just so-so).

Sometimes, **Ohima desuka?** (Do you have free time?) is used. This is the opening gambit when one is going to suggest, at the end of the working day, a game of mah jongg or some other leisure activity. But, for obvious reasons, during the working day it would be a big faux pas to ask a **mado-giwa-zoku** who appears to be idle, "**Ohima desuka?**"

See also Dochira-e?, Madogiwa-zoku, Mā-mā.

Okagesamade

"How is your child's injury?" "**Okagesamade** he has recovered completely and he is jumping around like before."

"How is business at your new branch store?"

"**Okagesamade** our sales have been good from the opening day."

Okagesamade is a word for expressing gratitude and means "Thanks to you."

The dialogue given above is between friends or

acquaintances and the persons asking the questions are not a doctor nor a banker. The Westerner would then wonder, "Why is it thanks to you?" But the "you" of "thanks to you" means "people in general, including you." And, the speaker is saying "You also have an **en** as a member of society together with the doctor who treated my child and the banker who lent me money to open the branch."

Thus, if in answer to a question the other party should say **Okagesamade** things went well," the appropriate response would be, "That's wonderful" or the like. If you should interpret this **okagesamade** as an expression of gratitude to you personally and say, "Not at all," the conversation will take an embarrassing turn. (Or, perhaps, because you are a **gaijin,** it might lead to good-natured laughter.

See also Go-en, Gaijin.

Okame-hachimoku

This term has its origin in the game of **go,** meaning that the observer of a match will be able to see eight (**hachi**) moves ahead although the contestants cannot. In other words, the expression means that a knowledgeable third party on the sidelines will be able to judge a situation with a cooler head than the parties who are completely absorbed in a matter.

One theory is that the meaning of the expression comes from the use of the word **oka** (hill), indicating that from a high place one can see the overall picture better. However, it seems that the meaning

of the term is rather "watching from the side."
Hachi is used here to mean "many."

Oka-bore means to fall in love with another person's wife or sweetheart.

Oka-yaki means to be jealous of another person's success in life. (**Yaku** = to be jealous)

Okappiki are ex-criminals and ex-gangsters who acted as police stool pigeons in the days of the Edo Shogunate.

In all these cases, **oka** is used in the meaning of "a third party."

OL

This is not a Japanese word; the **O** and the **L** are letters of the English alphabet and pronounced as such. The Japanese took the first letters of "office" and "lady" to coin the expression to mean young office girls.

During the high economic growth era, the Japanese began to use the term **bijinesu-man** (businessman) instead of the old **sararī-man** (salaried man) to refer to a corporate employee. Along with this, girl office workers were called **BG** (standing for "business girl"). But then, the Japanese learned that in some parts of the world "business girl" has an unsavory meaning. Its sound, too, was a bit harsh. So, in its place, **OL** was invented. Although the nuance of "unmarried" is strong in **OL**, it's reference is not restricted to single female clerks.

The point is, up to what age can female clerks be called **OL**? In general, **OL** are girls up to the marriageable age or just slightly above. If one were to call a female clerk who is obviously past forty an **OL**, it would be mutually embarrassing.

In recent years, an increasing number of women are getting into managerial positions. They are called "career women."

Ōmono

A truly outstanding leader is called **ōmono** or **daijinbutsu**. In Japan, however, the **ōmono** is not necessarily a man who stands at the top and guides or commands. A person who is called **ōmono** is one who delegates full authority to his deputy or chief of staff and takes responsibility for their actions.

Saigō Takamori, one of the architects of the Meiji Restoration, was typical of this kind of **ōmono**. Even though he died in the rebellion he instigated, he was able after death to recoup his honor and is regarded to this day by the nation as a hero.

The **ōmono** is a wise man who appears on the surface to be a fool. Therefore, if you should say to a person, "You are an **ōmono**," with the intention of praising him, that person will take it to mean "You are a fool" and will get angry. To say "—because he's an **ōmono**" could mean "Because he puts on the air of an **ōmono**, he won't take up such a small matter" or "He doesn't get disturbed by things, in other words, he is dull-witted, so he won't understand even if you tell him that." Both meanings are uncomplimentary. **Daijinbutsu** contains no uncomplimentary nuance. It refers simply to an outstanding **ōmono**.

See also Hiru-andon.

On

In the old days, when a feudal samurai received an **on** from a lord, he repaid the favor by offering his service (military service). In this case, the **on** was the bestowal of a fief. **On** is the act of bestowing on another person something (usually goods) that makes the receiver feel grateful and arouses in him a sense of obligation. If the thing bestowed is spiritual, it is called **nasake** or **jō** (compassion). Whichever the case, the receiver is obliged to return the favor, and this sense of obligation is **giri**.

Any act of bestowal that is obviously motivated by the expectation of a repayment becomes a not too laudable act of **on wo uru** (to sell **on**). When one forces another to feel obligated and seeks repayment it becomes an act of **on ni kiseru** (to fasten **on**).

When an obligation is repaid it is **on-gaeshi**. When a person neglects to repay a favor even when he is able to do so, he is criticized as **on-shirazu** (ignorant of **on**). When one returns kindness with ingratitude or bites the hand that feeds him, it is a depraved act described as ''**on wo ada de kaesu.**''

Oya no on (obligation to parents) is repaid by looking after parents in their old age.

See also Giri.

Onaji kama no meshi

This expression refers to people who have eaten rice (**meshi**) from the same (**onaji**) pot (**kama**). It is used to describe the relationship between people who are not of the same family but who have lived together for a period of time and shared the same experiences.

In most cases the relationship built up from sharing rice from the same pot is very close. Usually, the feeling of solidarity is maintained through life, and one can invariably count on such comrades for assistance and support. As a corollary, one finds it difficult to reject a request if he is reminded by the other pary, "Aren't we comrades who ate rice from the same pot?"

In order to create the feeling of comradeship, occasions are actually created for groups of people to eat from the same pot. Many companies put recruits under training in a dormitory or a retreat for a few days to a week to live together.

In Japanese society, where human relationship is all-important, everybody tries to belong to a group of one sort or another, and people welcome the experience of eating from the same pot.

See also Batsu, Jin-myaku.

Osumitsuki

This term originated in Japan's feudal days. It referred to a formal paper signed by the shogun, or feudal lord, certifying that the bearer had been granted a certain authority or privilege. It was a sort of credential that was absolute, coming as it did from the highest power in the land.

Today, the term is used in a popular and informal sense to indicate that a person or a thing has received a stamp of approval, guarantee, or support from some authoritative party.

A subordinate asks his manager about a promotion rumor. The superior says, "The rumor is correct. In the next personnel reassignment, I shall promote you to submanager." The subordinate can then say that he has received the **osumitsuki** of his superior. In such cases, the manager would not say he gives **osumitsuki;** it is the subordinate who says he receives it.

Otemori

This means "filling one's own plate or bowl with food from a pot" instead of having it filled by someone else. In the days when Japan was poor—up to about twenty to thirty years ago—getting enough to eat was a big problem, and it was human nature to try to put more food on one's own plate than on those of others.

The country having become more affluent and food of all kinds easily available, such a show of greediness is not seen any more at buffet parties. However, the tendency to take more of a good thing for oneself persists in other aspects of society. Such behavior is labeled **otemori,** even though it does not concern food. Thus, the expression describes the somewhat greedy or self-serving act of any person who is in a position to allocate by himself.

For instance, when legislators vote for themselves a big increase in remuneration, the public would criticize the action as **otemori.** This tendency to be generous to oneself is probably universal, but the English language does not seem to have a word that by itself expresses the third-party reaction as aptly as **otemori** does.

Ōwarawa

Ō means "big" or "great" and **warawa** means "a child." Up to the mid-nineteenth century, the front part of the head in the men's **chonmage** topknot hair style was shaved clean. The reason, it seems, was that this made it easier to put on the warrior's helmet. The topknot of the samurai engaged in fierce combat on the battlefield would become unraveled, and the long hair falling down to his shoulders looked like a child's hairstyle. From this came the word **ōwarawa,** meaning a big child.

The accountant battling with figures at the settling of accounts at the end of the business term and the housewife running around busily to put up decorations and prepare dishes for the New Year—both are **ōwarawa.** In other words, the word describes a person who is engaged so busily in a pressing task that he has no time to think about his appearance.

Although the Japanese consider it a virtue to be busy, they do not necessarily think that being **ōwarawa** at all times presents a pretty picture. If one disregards the pace of the entire work place and is **ōwarawa** all by himself, he will be described as **kara-mawari** (the phonograph disk continuing to revolve without a sound after the music is over).

See also Mōretsu, Oisogashii desuka?

Oyakata hinomaru

Oyakata is "godfather," boss, while **hinomaru** is the Japanese national flag. Thus, **oyakata hinomaru** refers to the Japanese government and carries the implication "free of care because the government will pick up the tab."

In the case of private companies struggling under fierce competition, those whose losses keep mounting eventually go bankrupt. But public corporations can afford to keep operating continuously at a loss, because in the end the government will look after them. Thus public corporations take it easy and neglect to make efforts. **Oyakata hinomaru** is a sarcastic reference to this kind of situation.

Even big private enterprises are sometimes sarcastically referred to as being the same as **oyakata hinomaru.** When a person from a parent company who has been assigned to become a director of a subsidiary is lavish in his expense account spending, the employees of the subsidiary would scornfully say, "He doesn't have to worry because of **oyakata hinomaru,**" implying that even if the subsidiary should go bankrupt, that director will be able to return to the parent company, whereas the employees of the subsidiary will become unemployed.

See also Ama-kudari, Tonosama shōbai.

Ringi

Ringi is the system of circulating an intraoffice memorandum (**ringi-sho**) to obtain the approval of all concerned for a proposed course of action, which could range from, say, the purchase of a word processor to a merger. Corporate decisions and actions seldom take place without **ringi.**

Depending on the nature of the proposal, the **ringi-sho** may circulate vertically from the bottom up or horizontally among managers and directors of related sections and divisions before coming up to the managing director or the president, depending on the importance of the subject matter. It goes without saying that **nemawashi** is necessary before the **ringi-sho** is circulated. Each person puts a seal (**hanko**) of approval on it, which is the Japanese equivalent of the signature in the Western world.

The advantage of this system is that everyone becomes involved so that once a decision has been made, companywide cooperation in its implementation is assured. Also, if anything goes wrong, responsibility is conveniently diffused so that nobody gets blamed.

See also Hanko, Nemawashi.

Rōnin

Rōnin were the samurai of feudal days who, for one reason or another, were not in the service of a lord. Thus the word is usually translated as ''masterless samurai.'' Today, a century after the samurai disappeared, there are still many **rōnin** in Japanese society.

One type of modern-day **rōnin** is the high school graduate who fails to pass a university entrance examination and studies privately before trying his luck again the following year. There are tens of thousands of such youngsters, some of whom have been **rōnin** for two or three years.

Another type of **rōnin** is the person who is unemployed, not because no company would hire him, but because he is particular about the kind of work he wants to do. Such a person is voluntarily unemployed. Politicians who have failed in an election and who are preparing to run in the next one are also called **rōnin**.

Sābisu

Although **sābisu** is adopted from the English word "service," the Japanese have given it the meaning "free," or "without charge" and "discount."

When the customer in a shop uses it as a verb, saying, "**Sābisu shite,**" he means, "Give me a discount." The clerk replies, "I can't make it any cheaper, but I'll **sābisu** this," and offers a novelty as a gift or gives an extra quantity of the thing being purchased. When slightly damaged fresh foodstuffs are sold at a big discount, it is labeled in red as **sābisu** item."

Of course, when one says of a restaurant or a bar "the **sābisu** is good/bad," the meaning is exactly the same as the original English "service." Sometimes one sees a sign outside a restaurant saying, "Today is **Sābisu** Day," but this does not mean that the service will be good on that particular day. It means that a cup of coffee will be presented free of charge if you order such and such a dish or that a small discount will be given on such and such a dish.

Saji wo nageru

In Japan when a person throws (**nageru**) a spoon (**saji**), he is neither fighting nor exhibiting a fit of bad temper. Figuratively, it means he has exhausted all means and has given up. The spoon referred to is the one doctors used to administer medicine to patients. When the patient's condition became hopeless and medicine had no more effect, the doctor threw in the towel or, rather, the spoon. In the business world, when negotiations come up against a stone wall and one side abandons further efforts, we say **saji wo nageru**. A businessman who tends to **saji wo nageru** too easily as soon as he comes up against a hard nut to crack will be criticized as lacking **konjō** (tenacity).

Another handy expression with the word spoon in it is **saji-kagen,** which means how much medicine will be put in a spoon. From this, the verb **saji-kagen wo suru** is used to mean ''making allowance for'' or ''using one's discretion in doing'' something.

See also Myaku, Konjō.

-San

The Japanese don't have to worry whether they should address a woman as Mrs. or Miss. The suffix **-san** is neuter and can be used for everybody. It can come after the family name, as in ''Tanaka-**san**'' or ''Smith-**san**'' or after the first name, as in ''Hanako-**san**'' or ''Mary-**san,**'' although Japanese men do not call each other by the first name. Sometimes, it can be inconvenient because upon meeting Tanaka-**san,** you suddenly discover it's a she and not a he as you thought all along.

The suffix **-san** is also used with company names: ''Mitsubishi-**san.**'' A superior usually does not call his subordinate **-san.** Nor do close friends address each other as **-san.** The suffix they use is **-kun.** Women friends, however, do not call each other **-kun.**

In a business organization, persons with titles are usually addressed only by their title, such as **buchō** (manager) or **shachō** (president). It is not only in the office that this form of address is used. At year-end parties and on the golf course, too, people are addressed by their title. This may sound to people of the West like failing to draw a line between private and public life, but in Japan it is the accepted etiquette. This is because in the old days it was considered impolite to call a person by name.

See also Bureikō.

Sasen

This is the act of being demoted or being transferred to a regional office, although one's rank is not lowered.

In Japan, it is rare for an employed worker to be dismissed **(kubi ni naru)** for such reasons as bungling a job or not getting along with his superior. However, quite often a section chief may be given an assignment in which his rank is not changed but he has no subordinates under him. Or, he may be shifted from a section chief's post in the head office to that in a branch. This is called **sasen,** which means "lowering the seating order."

The transferring of an employee to a small branch or a local office in an isolated place is known as **tobasu** (send flying). It's a good feeling to send a golf ball flying, but when a person himself is sent

flying, he realizes that he has been shunted off the promotion course. It is a case of **miyako-ochi** (being sent away from the center of power to the provinces). This is sometimes described also as **shima-nagashi** (banished to an isolated island). At any rate, **sasen** is the most feared word in the corporate employee's lexicon.
See also Dosa-mawari, Kubi, Madogiwa-zoku.

Seifuku

Tellers, typists, secretaries, and all other female employees of banks work in company-provided uniforms—**seifuku.** So do girls with securities brokerages, insurance companies, department stores, and supermarkets. Almost all girls working in large Japanese companies wear uniforms in either offices or factories.

Of the top 2,000 Japanese companies, there are very few that do not provide uniforms for girls. But there are very few companies that provide uniforms for white-collar male employees; they wear company badges on their suit lapels.

In the belief that the company uniform plays an important role in corporate image-making, more and more companies are using top designers, including such international big names as Hanae Mori, to design their uniforms. This pleases the girls.

Seiri-kyūka

This is a special menstrual leave for women workers under the Labor Standards Law. The spirit of the law is to relieve women workers from having to work with the additional burden of a physiological discomfort. Because there are individual differences in the degree of discomfort and in the heaviness of duties, there are people who complain that the **seiri-kyūka** system is unfair.

Male corporate employees also have **seiri-kyūka,** thanks not to the provisions of the law but to corporate magnanimity. When they are transferred to distant cities, many corporate employees leave their families behind and go off on their own. This is called **tanshin-funin.** Once or twice a month, the **tanshin-funin** worker gets a leave **(kyūka)** to return to his home carrying a bagful of soiled underwear, socks, etc. This leave is jestingly called the men's **seiri-kyūka.**

Some companies are even so considerate as to send the **tanshin-funin** worker once in two or three months on a business trip **(shutchō)** to an office or branch close to his home. Nobody calls this a **seiri-shutchō,** but it is one of the ways that the company displays its concern for the employee's welfare.

See also Chon, Tanshin-funin.

Sekigahara, Ten·nōzan

The battles of **Sekigahara** (1600) and **Ten·nōzan** (1582) were, like the Battle of Waterloo, decisive battles that changed the course of history.

Whereas Waterloo is used to mean a crushing defeat, the emphasis of the Japanese names is on a crucial contest or critical dividing point in the course of events. It was said that a person who emerges victorious in **Sekigahara** or **Ten·nōzan** becomes the ruler of **tenka,** or all Japan.

The Japanese, who have a penchant for dramatizing things, are very fond of using these terms in describing any kind of confrontation. The final decisive negotiations between management and labor union on a pay increase is referred to as a **Ten· nōzan.** A struggle between two companies for domination of a market is termed a **Sekigahara.**

Sekiji

Sekiji means the seating order at a formal function. This is something that also exists in the Western society. In addition, **sekiji** refers to the order of rank in an organization such as a company. The person whose **sekiji** in the company is higher sits closer to the head of the table at parties also.

In Japanese society, where the seniority system is the rule, generally the person who is older has a higher **sekiji.** If two persons have the same rank in the company, the person who rose to that rank earlier in point of time usually has a higher **sekiji.**

See also Bureikō, Dōki.

Senpai and Kōhai

In the Japanese business world, one of the gambits used to influence a person is to approach him through his **senpai. Senpai** is a person who has preceded another in graduating from school, in joining a company or government service, in assuming a post, in acquiring an experience, etc. **Kō-**

hai is someone who follows in the footsteps of the **senpai**.

In Japan's seniority-conscious and paternalistic society, the **senpai-kōhai** relationship is of great importance. The **senpai** looks after the interests of the **kōhai**, and the latter seeks help and advice from the former and respects his wishes.

A generation or so ago, the **senpai–kōhai** relationship was viable if the two sides had never met previously. Nowadays, there is a perceptible dilution of the relationship in the cases where the two are not already acquainted with each other personally.

See also Dōki, Jin-myaku.

Sensei

The two characters that make up this word mean "ahead, first" (**sen**) and "to be born" (**sei**). It is the term of respect used to refer to other people. In China, the word used to be a form of address before it was replaced by the current **ton-chi** (comrade).

Sensei is used to address a wide variety of people ranging from school teachers, physicians, and lawyers to athletic coaches and instructors of flower arrangement and other cultural attainments. In the classroom, the pupil will never call a teacher by name; it is always **sensei**. In Japan, it is considered impolite for a pupil to address a teacher as "Mr. so-and-so" or "Miss so-and-so."

Members of parliament don't like it unless you call them **sensei**. Of course, when they fail in an election, they become merely "Mr. so-and-so."

However, the word is often used ironically with a feeling of contempt. In "That **sensei** is always making blunders" the word would mean "stupid fellow." In "Hey, **sensei** over there, pass me the box of matches," the nuance is "slow-witted fellow."

Thus, **sensei** is a word influenced in its meaning by TPO (time, place and occasion).

See also Keiko, -San.

Shafū

Sha stands for **kaisha** (company), while **fū** is the Chinese phonetic reading of the character that stands for "wind." In this case, **fū** stands for "manners, customs, practice, style, mood."

Shafū is a sort of unwritten and tacitly understood code of behavior for a company's employees. It is not in the form of written rules stipulating how employees should conduct themselves. For instance, one can say, "The **shafū** in our company is such that marriage between employees is not welcomed."

The word is sometimes used to mean what is referred to in the West as corporate identity or corporate image. Loosely, it is the impression of the company which employees give to outsiders through their behavior. "It seems that company's enthusiasm for developing new products is its **shafū**." "The salesmen of that company behave as if they are doing you a favor by selling you goods. It must be the company's **shafū**."

Similarly, there is a **ka** (family) **-fū**. This is a word all mothers-in-law like to use in making their son's wife conform to their ways: ''This is our **ka-fū,** so please get used to it quickly.

See also Sha-nai, Tonosama shōbai.

Shain-ryō, Tanshin-ryō

Large Japanese companies maintain dormitories called **shain-ryō** for their employees. Multistory dormitories for bachelor employees whose family homes are outside the city are known as **tanshin-ryō.**

Companies with many branches or facilities in various cities throughout the country maintain dormitories in each location to house employees transferred from another city.

The use of dormitories is voluntary, and each company has its own regulations on the qualifications for occupancy. The communal dormitory life helps to generate affinity among the employees. The dormitory fee, usually a nominal sum, is deducted from the monthly pay.

Some companies provide independent housing units for families, which are called **sha-taku.**

See also -Chon, Tanshin-funin.

Shain-ryokō

Shain-ryokō is one of the methods used in Japanese companies to strengthen group consciousness. It is the company excursion in which all executives and employees are expected to participate. In a large company, the excursion is held in divisional or even smaller groups so that all members can be accommodated at the same resort inn.

The main event is a big banquet where drinks flow freely and break down reserves. The informal atmosphere gives junior employees and secretaries a chance to talk and kid with their bosses. The party is enlivened by singing, impromptu skits, and the like, with each person contributing some kind of performance. At night some of the participants, sometimes even a dozen or more, sleep side by side in the same room on the **tatami** (straw matting). On the following day, they usually go sightseeing.

See also Bureikō, Kakushi-gei.

Shain-shokudō

Most large Japanese companies have within their premises a subsidized cafeteria where employees can eat lunch at prices considerably lower than in outside restaurants. Some **shain-shokudō** offer a wide variety of dishes, Japanese, Chinese, and Western. The modest ones offer only snack type food.

In addition to being cheap, the **shain-shokudō** is convenient for those who are pressed for time and must take a quick lunch. Not only the rank-and-file but also the managers and executives use the same company cafeteria. Usually, a catering company operates the cafeteria under the company's supervision.

Shaka

The story is told that an early morning Western visitor to a world-famous Japanese corporation was astounded at the sight of assembled employees singing the **shaka** (company anthem) before starting the day's work. Not many companies go through this ritual, but quite a few companies have their own songs.

They are sung in chorus on such occasions as the first day of the year, the company anniversary, and the opening of a new branch office. The **shaka** enhances the sense of belonging in much the same way as the uniforms of blue-collar and female workers and company badges worn by white-collar workers on their suit lapels.

Many companies also have corporate flags. Some Japanese companies have experimented with modern American corporate identity programs, but they have found that the traditional methods are more effective for Japanese workers.

See also Chōrei.

Sha-nai

The Japanese company is a community in itself and likes to draw a clear line between what is inside the company (**sha-nai**) and what is outside (**sha-gai**). As a noun, **sha-nai** is used in exactly the same way as the English "the inside." But in the adjectival meaning of in-company or intramural, it is probably used in more ways than its English equivalents.

We have **sha-nai yokin** (in-company savings), which is a system under which a part of the employee's pay is checked off as savings deposited with the company at a higher interest rate than the usual city bank interest on deposits. Then there is the **sha-nai ryokō,** which is a company excursion. There is also **sha-nai kekkon** (in-company wedding), which is the term applied when a man and a woman who work/worked in the same company get married. **Sha-nai kekkon,** of course, is not a system, but when co-workers do decide to get married, the ceremony tends to become an affair celebrated by the whole company community.

Japanese companies put on documents the stamp **sha-gai-hi** (outside-company secret), which actually means "to be kept secret within the company."

See also Shain-ryokō, Shain shokudō.

Shayō-zoku

When this word is directly translated, it doesn't make sense, because it comes out as "company business tribe." It refers to corporate employees who are privileged to live it up at the company's expense. The impression the word conveys is "expense-account plutocrats."

These are people holding positions that require them to do a lot of business entertaining and therefore have fat expense accounts. They are the best customers of plush restaurants, nightclubs, and bars. In fact, the business of many such establishments is solely dependent on the **shayō-zoku.**

These people are usually envied, but they can be an unhappy tribe when they are reassigned and return to paying out of their own wallets like other salaried employees.

See also Kōsai-hi.

Shaze, Shakun

Most Japanese companies have either a **shaze** or a **shakun** or both. **Sha** means company. **Ze** means what is right or justification. **Kun** means precept. **Shaze** means, therefore, a statement of corporate principles and ideals, and loosely corresponds to the motto of a Western corporation. **Shakun** is a statement of basic precepts or exhortations directed at company employees.

Shaze is usually tersely expressed in lofty, high-sounding, formalized language. **Shakun** sometimes takes the same form but is more often expressed in ordinary language.

The original is usually written in brush calligraphy, framed, and hung in the president's office or the board room. At some companies, it is customary for the employees to recite the **shaze** or **shakun** in unison every morning before starting work.

See also Chōrei.

Shin·nyū-shain

April is the month in which companies welcome into their fold the new crop of high school and university graduates. Although graduation is in spring, the recruits, known as **shin·nyū-shain,** are almost all chosen by the end of the preceding year in the process known as **aota-gai.**

Every company holds a formal ceremony to welcome the recruits, with the president giving a speech to tell them what is expected of them and what they can expect from the company during their lifetime employment.

The recruits are then given a course of basic training during which the company spirit is hammered into them and they learn the general outline of the company's business. This training lasts anywhere from a week to a couple of months, depending on the company. In some cases, they enter a company retreat, where they eat and sleep together to cement **dōki** ties. After the training period, they are assigned to various sections for on-the-job training to learn specific business skills.

See also Aota-gai, Dōki.

Shintai-ukagai

This is a unique Japanese device for smoothly settling a matter that otherwise could become very messy. It shows the Japanese genius for avoiding unpleasant consequences for all concerned and solving a problem without damaging reputations.

An employee who has caused a big loss to his company or has acted in a dishonorable way in his private life, thus bringing about the possibility of tarnishing his company's image, writes a letter to his superior asking whether he should resign. In other words, he admits he did wrong and tells the company that he is prepared to take responsibility and resign if the company thinks that is best.

In principle, the person concerned submits the **shintai-ukagai** of his own free will. In some cases, he is urged by his superiors or colleagues to do so on the unspoken understanding that if he should do so he would not be asked to take responsibility or that he might be given only a light punishment of, say, suspension of pay raise for one year. This is because in Japanese society a voluntarily expressed remorse is always rewarded with magnanimous treatment.

See also Jirei.

Shio

In the sixteenth century, during the age of civil strife in Japan, the inland territory of feudal lord Takeda Shingen was placed under an economic blockade by two enemy warlords whose territories faced the sea. One of the commodities the blockaded force lacked was salt (**shio**), because in those days the only source of salt in Japan was sea water. At such a time, enemy general Uesugi Kenshin sent some salt to the besieged forces. This act was applauded as a display of the samurai's sense of fair play—"Let's fight on an equal footing." Thus, the expression **teki ni shio wo okuru** (send salt to the enemy) was used to mean an act of fair play.

Today, however, it has changed to mean "benefiting the enemy" and is used in such ways as "to export arms to that country is just like sending salt to the enemy."

Salt is used in Japan for purification. When **sumō** wrestlers enter the ring, they grab a fistful of salt and sprinkle it on the ring to cleanse it of impurities. When a customer misbehaves or tells an unlucky story in a drinking establishment, the hostess will sprinkle salt after that customer when he leaves.

Shiraha-no-ya

Shiraha is white feather, and **ya** is arrow. The full expression is **shiraha-no-ya ga tatsu** or **shiraha-no-ya wo tateru.**

There are many legends in Japan about gods who demand human offerings. One legend tells about a god who shoots a white-feathered arrow on the roof of the home where the girl he desires as an offering lives. Thus, **shiraha-no-ya** was originally used in the tragic sense of being selected as a sacrifice from among a large number of people. Today, however, the expression is used mainly in the happier sense that a person has been singled out for a responsible duty from among many other candidates.

However, because the expression's original nuance still persists, it is not used in congratulating a person directly in such a way as, "Congratulations for the **shiraha-no-ya** falling on you as the manager of the new project." Out of the selected man's earshot, his colleagues would use the expression, putting into it mixed feelings of sympathy for being given a difficult assignment and a touch of envy.

Shiri

In Japan, there are so many expressions which use the word **shiri** (buttocks, hips) that one can almost write an anecdote in which the word appears in every sentence.

For instance: "My business partner is **shiri ga omoi** (literally, **shiri** is heavy) and he did not get down to work until **shiri ni hi ga tsuku** (his **shiri** caught on fire). Finally, he **shiri wo makutte shimatta** (lifted up his kimono hem to reveal his **shiri**) and **shiri ga mochikomareta** (**shiri** was brought in) to me, his partner. Eventually, I had to **shiri-nugui** (wipe the **shiri**) for him.''

The explanation: **shiri ga omoi** = slow to get started in work; **shiri ni hi ga tsuki** = driven by necessity; **shiri wo makuru** = assume a defiant attitude; **shiri wo mochikomu** = ask another person to set right matters which have gone wrong; **shiri-nugui** = fix things up after another person has bungled them.

Among the many other **shiri** expressions, those it would be tactful to avoid saying in the presence of the fair sex are **teishu wo shiri ni shiku** (henpeck), and **shiri ga karui** (used of a wanton woman), and **shirino anaga chiisai** (timid, fainthearted).

See also Koshi.

Shita, Kuchi

For some reason, many of the Japanese expressions associated with man's tongue (**shita**) and mouth (**kuchi**) do not have a complimentary tone. For instance, there is the **nimai-jita** (double-tongued) person whose words cannot be trusted because he is a double-dealer or a liar.

Kuchi-guruma ni noseru (loosely: take a person on a ride on one's mouth wheel) is to take a person in with sweet talk.

Kōzetsu no to, where **kō** is the phonetic reading of the character for mouth and **zetsu** that for tongue, is a person who talks so much that he causes controversy.

Shitasaki-sanzun (tip of the tongue three inches) describes a person with a smooth tongue who usually uses it to explain away his mistake or failure glibly.

A complimentary expression using the word mouth is **kuchi hattchō te hattchō** (skillful with the mouth, skillful with the hand). This refers to a person who is voluble and eloquent as well as efficient in doing things.

If a person does something in an exceptional way, he makes people **shita wo maku** (roll up the tongue), or astonishes them.

A modern expression which is a good example of the ingenious way the Japanese adapt and assimilate foreign words is **kuchi-komi. Komi** is a corruption of the English word communication. Thus, the combination of Japanese and corrupted English translates as "mouth communication" or "by word of mouth."

Shitsurei shimasu

Shitsurei shimasu is a very convenient expression for a foreign resident in Japan to learn. It is a polite expression which is used in those situations and occasions when in English a person would say, "excuse me, but—," "by your leave—," "with your permission—," "with all due respect to you—," "allow me to take the liberty," "sorry to interrupt you." A visitor can use it both on entering and on leaving somebody else's office.

It is also used in an entirely different context to mean simply "good-bye" or "well, I must be going now." In this second meaning, **shitsurei shimasu** is used more often than **sayonara** in everyday situations by the person who is taking leave. However, when you are saying good-bye at the airport upon your departure, **sayonara** is the word.

See also Kekkō desu, Dōmo.

Shukkō-shain

In Japan, the mobility of white-collar workers is very low. When people join a company, they intend normally to stay with that company until the compulsory retirement age. But sometimes the management temporarily assigns an employee to work in another company. Such an employee is called a **shukkō-shain.**

Usually he works on a loan basis, with the understanding that he will be given the chance of returning to his original company. However, some persons choose to stay with the new company for the rest of their lives.

Senior executives are loaned to subsidiaries for support purposes. Banks loan executives as finance officers to companies they finance. Manufacturers loan sales engineers to distributors. Central government agencies loan officials to local government agencies and industry associations.

One might say that the **shukkō-shain** system is a sort of substitute for the executive recruiting normal in other countries.

See also Ama-kudari.

Shuntō

In spring (the character for **shun** is also read as **haru** = spring) Japanese labor unions traditionally conduct a struggle (**tō**) for a wage increase and improvement of various labor conditions.

Sohyo (one of the two biggest labor federations in Japan, the other being Domei) carried out the first **shuntō** in 1955. In the initial years, only a few unions took part, but gradually more and more joined until **shuntō** became the biggest annual event in labor–management relations.

The **shuntō** formula was Sohyo's brainchild for making up for the weakness of Japanese labor unions, which are organized on an enterprise basis. The formula makes it possible for a large number of small unions to conduct collective bargaining for wage increases on an industrywide basis although they are not organized as industrial unions.

Wage increases do not seem directly to trigger price increases. This is probably because there is a tacit understanding between unions and management that the rate of wage increase would be kept below the rate of increase in productivity.

Shūshin-koyō

Much has been said about the advantages—both to the company and to the employee—of the Japanese lifetime employment (**shūshin-koyō**) system. Although the system offers security to the worker, it also makes it extremely difficult for a person to change his employment.

For the individual, it is vitally important to join a

good company upon graduation from school. For management, it is vitally important to secure good-quality people who will be useful for the next thirty-five years or so. This means that the competition to recruit and to gain admission to a company is very severe.

The era of low-growth economy has begun to expose one of the drawbacks of the lifetime employment system. Companies having to keep on their payroll old employees whose salaries are high but whose usefulness has declined are beginning to suffer. Thus the **kibō-taishoku** system has been introduced.

See also Teiki-saiyō, Kibō-taishoku, Teinen.

Sode-no-shita

When a person gives money **sode-no-shita,** he is doing so ''under-the-sleeve''—furtively, secretly, underhandedly. Thus, it is the Japanese counterpart of ''under-the-table.'' To bribe a person is **sode-no-shita wo tsukau.** To accept a bribe is **sode-no-shita wo morau** or **ukeru.** To be corruptible or bribable is **sode-no-shita no kiku.**

Japanese government officials are said to be hard to bribe. Thus, when a case of bribery is exposed, even though it may be a small case involving an insignificant sum of money, it is usually given big play by the mass media.

The accepted Japanese way of expressing appreciation for special favors received is to send gifts in the traditional gift-giving seasons of **ochū-gen** (midsummer) and **oseibo** (year-end).

Soko wo nantoka

Sometimes a businessman has to engage in difficult negotiations. The more he listens to the other side's explanations and arguments, the more hopeless his own case seems to become. The face of his boss flits before his eyes, and he realizes that he can't go back to him with the kind of conditions laid down by the other side.

At such a time, the words that come out of his mouth are "**soko wo nantoka—**." **Soko** means "that" and in this case it is a reference to the stated position, conditions, or contention of the other party. **Nantoka** is a vague way of saying "please ease or moderate your conditions" or "please accept even a small part of our conditions." It carries the meaning of "please be a little more conciliatory so that we could somehow find a way to reach agreement."

Greater stress is put into the appeal by inserting the word **magete** (bend): **soko wo magete nantoka—**.

This expression is frequently used in Japanese society, which doesn't take to rational, businesslike negotiation so readily.

See also Naki.

Sōritsu-kinenbi

Japanese companies attach importance to the anniversary of their foundation (**sōritsu-kinenbi**). Big milestones, such as the tenth, twentieth, twenty-fifth, fiftieth, and so on, are usually celebrated with a big anniversary party.

The president makes a speech to thank suppliers, contractors, banks, and employees for their help and support in making the company what it is. The company song and three shouts of **banzai** (Long live the company!) conclude the formal ceremony. Then employees and guests are served **sake,** the rice wine, and the festive red bean rice. Shareholders receive a bonus dividend.

In recent years it has become fashionable to publish the company history on big anniversaries. Not uncommon today is the substitution of an employee athletic meet or a special paid leave for the formal ceremony.

See also Shaka.

Soroban

Before the advent of the electronic calculator, the abacus (**soroban**) was in the attaché case of the Japanese businessman as he traveled all over the world buying raw materials or selling manufactured goods. The abacus made the Japanese wizards at adding, subtracting, multiplying, and dividing figures of multiple digits.

The assumption that the electronic calculator and computer have made the abacus a museum piece is given the lie by the fact that in 1981 there were more than 10,000 private **soroban** schools run mostly by individuals, an increase of more than 3,000 in five years, and that hundreds of thousands of youngsters take the annual examinations to obtain the official **soroban** accounting certificate of the Japan Chamber of Commerce.

The operation of the abacus is regarded as good

not only for developing mathematical ability but also for general mental training. The word **soroban** is used in a number of expressions to mean profitable, mercenary, commercially minded, etc.

Sumimasen

This is the Japanese equivalent of "I'm sorry" or "Excuse me." Although the original sense of the word is an expression of apology for having done something wrong, it has several other common uses.

It can be used to draw the attention of a person when you don't know his name. Addressing a waitress to place an order or addressing someone in the street to ask for directions is a typical use of **sumimasen.** It can also be used as an informal "Thank you."

Sumimasen sometimes means "Please" when asking someone to do something. Suppose you visit someone at his office, you might say to the receptionist, "**Sumimasen** (Excuse me), I'd like to see Mr. Hara." "**Sumimasen** (Please) show me how to get to his office." "**Sumimasen** (Thank you)" and then to Mr. Hara, "**Sumimasen** (Sorry) I kept you waiting."

See also Dōmo, Chotto.

Sune-kajiri

One often hears people talking about a young man who is "gnawing at (his father's) shins" (**sune-kajiri**). It means that the young man, who is old enough to earn his own living, is still dependent financially on his father.

A couple of generations ago, when Japanese wages were still very low, it was difficult for a young man just out of school to live on his starting pay. In those days **sune-kajiri** was quite common and not a stigma.

As Japan became economically affluent, starting wages rose, and today young men just starting work receive enough pay to cover their own living expenses. Thus the new breed of **sune-kajiri** sons are those who do not take up an occupation after graduating from school but pursue some special study or those who spend their wages for play and depend on their father for meals and a roof over their heads.

Suri-awase

If one should thoughtlessly place a new Japanese teacup or bowl on the table, it could result in a scratch on the surface of the table. This is because the rim on the underside of chinaware is not glazed. Therefore, whenever Japanese housewives buy new chinaware they rub the bottoms of two bowls together to smooth their rims. This process is called **suri-awase.**

From this, the word is used to describe the process of adjusting different viewpoints among members of a group through mutual concessions in order to coordinate and unify the opinion of the group as a whole. Similarly, the adjustment of views between different groups is also sometimes

called **suri-awase.** The former can also be called **nemawashi,** and the latter may be described as "bargaining." At any rate, the prerequisite is that differences are not too great, as can be presumed from the fact that the term originally means rubbing the bottoms of the same kind of bowl.

The word is used also in political circles for adjusting views within the same party, but it is not applicable to the diplomatic world.

See also Nemawashi.

Tadaima

This is a word used in everyday situations, but in two different meanings.

First, it is a word of greeting spoken by a person who returns to his home or office from the outside. In a way, it is an announcement meaning "I'm back." The full expression is "**tadaima kaeri-mashita**" (just now, I have returned). Those within hearing distance will reply, "**okaeri-nasai**" (welcome back). Some companies require their staffs to use these expressions as a matter of office etiquette.

The other way in which the word is used is in response to a request to "come here, Mr. so and so," or to do something. The **tadaima** in such a case means "Right away" or "I'll attend to it at once."

The place where one hears it most often is in small drinking establishments and restaurants. The customer sings out, "Another jug of beer, please!" The bartender or waitress responds "**tadaima**" (coming right up, sir). But it doesn't come right up, so the customer repeats his request. The answer this time may be "Yes, **tadaima, tadaima.**" When the **tadaima** is repeated in this way, the customer will do well to resign himself to slow service.

Taigū

Taigū is treatment, entertainment, and the degree of such treatment. When one is treated by a business acquaintance to a magnificent dinner and given red-carpet treatment, making him feel as if he had become a king, he would say, "Yesterday evening I received a king's **taigū.**"

"The **taigū** at that store was unbelievably good" would mean simply that the service was excellent. It might have been that the store had mistaken the person for someone of high rank.

Sometimes a businessman's visiting card would state his title as "Manager (or whatever) **taigū.**" This means that he has the rank equivalent to manager, etc. His salary, rank, and status are all equal to that of manager. In such cases, usually that person has a title but no subordinates under him.

With the economy in a period of low growth, Japanese corporations cannot increase the number of managerial posts. Yet, under the **nenkō-joretsu** system, they have to raise people to higher posts as they grow older. The **taigū** title was conceived to get around this dilemma.

See also Meishi, Nenkō-joretsu, Sābisu.

Tamamushi-iro

Tamamushi is a species of beetle (sometimes called jewel beetle) about 4 centimeters long whose distinguishing feature is its metallic iridescence caused by two lengthwise bars on its wing, one of which is golden green and the other golden purple. This beautiful wing has been used since olden times in artistic craftwork.

The color (**iro**) of this beetle's wing glows gold, green, red, purple, and blue, depending on the angle from which it is seen. Thus, it is brilliant but one is not sure what its actual color is. Thus, **tamamushi-iro** is used to describe an attitude or statement which could be interpreted in two or more ways.

Politicians answering opposition questions in the Diet (Japan's parliament) are famous for their **tamamushi-iro** answers. One is never sure whether they are in favor of or opposed to a certain idea. Gobbledygook can be classed as **tamamushi-iro.**

When something is neither black nor white, it is called **hai-iro** (color of ash = gray). **Hai-iro** refers to that which is absolutely and manifestly not clear, whereas **tamamushi-iro** refers to the subjective re-action of the listener and could differ and change relatively. Thus, the two expressions are not synonymous.

Tanabota

This is a contraction of the saying **tana kara bota-mochi ga ochite kita** (delicious cake fell from the shelf), meaning "visited by unexpected good fortune." It can be understood as the Japanese counterpart of "manna from heaven"—a godsend, a windfall. An uncle who went abroad and whose whereabouts was unknown passes away and leaves a big inheritance for you—this is **tanabota**. This kind of windfall is also known as **tanabota-shiki** good fortune.

A sudden demand arose for a product which was lying asleep in the warehouse, bringing big profit to the company and an unexpected special bonus to the employees. A **madogiwa-zoku** whose compulsory retirement age was just around the corner was suddenly appointed to the board of directors, and his life in the company was prolonged considerably. These are **tanabota-shiki** good fortune.

The proverb **kahō wa nete mate** (wait in bed for good fortune), which is similar to the saying that when one woke up in the morning he found that he had become famous overnight, may have its source in waiting for **tanabota**. After all, everyone dreams of **tanabota**.

See also Madogiwa-zoku.

Tana-oroshi

Here is a word which should be in the vocabulary of any foreign businessman selling goods in Japan. Literally meaning to take down (**oroshi**) from the shelf (**tana**), it is the Japanese term for stocktaking or inventory making. Book inventory is **chōbo-tana-oroshi;** inventory loss is **tana-oroshi-zon**.

The original meaning of taking down from the shelf and making an accounting has been twisted in social usage to mean "find faults, pick holes, run down, criticize, disparage." The favorite pastime of many men is to subject members of the fair sex to **tana-oroshi**.

Tanshin-funin

Tanshin-funin means "going to another city or country, unaccompanied by one's family, in order to take up a new post." **Tanshin-funin** is very common among middle-aged Japanese businessmen with children of high school age. Under the Japanese educational system, it is extremely disadvantageous for a boy or girl already in a high school to change schools. Thus, the father who is posted to a place away from home leaves his family behind and lives the life of a bachelor.

One might say that **tanshin-funin** is a description of a **"business bachelor."** The term is not used for an unmarried person. Some corporations are understanding enough to give the "business bachelor" a special allowance to maintain a separate household.

See also -Chon, Shain-ryō.

Tarai-mawashi

This is an acrobatic stunt in which a man lies flat on his back, raises his legs to support and twirl (**mawashi**) a **tarai** (wooden washtub 90–120 cm in diameter and 30 cm deep) with his feet.

From this, the expression is used to mean a situation in which things go around in circles without any basic change.

The **tarai-mawashi** of political power occurs when a party that perennially enjoys an absolute majority in parliament rotates the premiership among leaders of its own party and does not relinquish the post to a rival party.

A typical case of **tarai-mawashi** is experienced by many citizens when they go to the municipal office to lodge a complaint. The first official he approaches tells him, "This is not the section for that. Go to X section." There, you are again told, "Not here. X section handles it." Around and around you go, and that's **tarai-mawashi.** The same thing happens when you go to a physician and are told, "For your sickness, the best place is the X hospital." These are cases of evading responsibility.

Then there is the **tarai-mawashi** of the **ochūgen** and **oseibo** gifts one receives. What you receive from Mr. A, you present to Mr. B.

Tataki-age

The original meaning is to hammer metal, including the sword, into shape while it is in annealable condition. From this, it came to be used to mean the building of a man of sterling character and ability through continuous hard training. It is used of a person who rises from a lowly position, overcoming hardships and constantly struggling to better himself. A **tataki-age** person is highly respected because he succeeded in reaching the top through his own hard effort.

Somewhat similar, but different, are **nari-agari** and **nari-kin.** These words refer to a person who has suddenly made a big success or a big fortune. These two terms do not connote that success or fortune was achieved through solid effort. The nuance is that the achievement was a result of a stroke of good fortune or some not too respectable dealings.

Therefore there is a hint of scorn in the words **nari-agari** and **nari-kin**.

The same person who succeeded in life could be described by some as **tataki-age** and by others as **nari-agari**, expressing praise in the case of the former and jealousy or scorn for his good luck in the case of the latter. This depends on the subjective assessment of the observer.

Tataki-dai

Tataki-dai is a tentative proposal or a draft plan which serves as the basis for a discussion, as in "Let's study this subject together by using this proposal as the **tataki-dai**."

An indispensable part of a festival in Japan is the merchant who constantly and spiritedly pounds (**tataku** = verb form of **tataki**) on the table (**dai**) on which his wares are displayed in an effort to get customers to buy. Each time he pounds on the table, usually with a stick, he lowers his price a notch. The customers watch to see how far the price will go down before they buy.

Tataku took on the extended meaning of "to bruise, attack, grill (question intensively), and beat down the price."

A proposal is placed on the table and subjected to **tataki**—scrutinized from many angles, criticized, compared with alternatives.

The use of this word in this way started in the 1960s. Therefore, only the latest Japanese language dictionaries list it.

See also Benkyō.

Te

Being the part of the body which is the most useful to man, **te** (hand) figures in a great number of expressions.

When you diversify and start a new line of business it is **atarashī shōbai ni** (new business) **te wo tsukeru.** To conduct that new business you take steps (**te wo utsu**) such as obtaining a bank loan or recruiting personnel. It means taking a move to ensure that a necessary thing will be done. **Te wo utsu** can also mean strike a deal or close a purchase or negotiate a sale. **Te wo hiku** is withdraw (for instance from a deal).

In drawing up a contract, you make sure that there is no **te-ochi** (slip, careless error, oversight). If something goes wrong with the contract, it will be your **te-ochi** (your fault, your blame).

In negotiations, you try to find out the other side's **te no uchi** (inside of the palm = intentions) before you show your hand (**te no uchi wo miseru**). If the other party is obstinate, unreasonable and uncompromising, he is **te ni amaru** (too much for the hand = intractable, unmanageable). So you throw up your hands in dismay (**o-te-age**) which can mean to give up or to be at a loss what to do. Experiencing so much difficulty or trouble (**te wo yaku**), you might want to **te wo kiru** (cut off the hand = stop dealing with, cut off connections) with that party.

In manufacturing, your product for the Japanese market, it is best that you do not **te wo nuku**, because the Japanese consumer is very particular. It means ''cut corners'' in its bad sense—economize on labor, be careless, or skip over a process.

Teate

The monthly salary of most Japanese corporate employees consists of two parts—the so-called basic pay and the various allowances, which are called **teate**. A list of the various types of **teate** would easily fill this page.

Some are based on the employee's private situation (allowance for dependents, housing allowance, etc.). Some are pegged to work (allowance for holding responsible or managerial posts, allowance for being an operator of a certain piece of equipment, overtime allowance, nightwork allowance, etc.).

This system makes it seem that the **teate** is something extra, over and above the regular pay. In practice, however, both employees and employers think of the **teate** as part of the monthly salary. Evidence of this is the general trend towards discontinuing the custom of breaking down the payment into basic pay and allowances and lumping them together as the monthly pay.

Teiki-saiyō, Chūto-saiyō

Japanese corporations make it a practice to recruit workers regularly once a year in spring, the time when high schools and universities graduate their students. This annual hiring is called **teiki-saiyō**. The big corporations take in hundreds of graduates at the same time.

The hiring policy is not necessarily based on the need to fill a vacancy or to employ people to undertake specific tasks. How many people to hire is determined by each company's long-term strategic considerations.

If a company should find it necessary to hire people outside of the **teiki-saiyō** process, the form adopted is called **chūto-saiyō** (midway hiring). This may occur when a person with specialized know-how is suddenly needed or when a company expands its operations and needs a large number of experienced people at once.

See also Shin•nyū-shain, Hikinuki.

Teinen

Strictly speaking, the Japanese lifetime employment system does not guarantee lifelong employment. Employment terminates at the ages of fifty-five, fifty-seven or sixty, depending on each company's employment regulations, whereas the average life expectancy of the Japanese male is up to the mid-seventies. When the employee reaches the age for compulsory retirement (**teinen**), he automatically loses his job, regardless of his physical and mental condition or ability.

Until a decade or so ago, fifty-five was the universal compulsory retirement age, but corporations have been raising the retirement age gradually. While some have gone as high as sixty, those who are sticking to the old age limit still outnumber the others.

The retiring employee receives a lump sum retirement allowance and, with the government pension program, usually can live without too much financial worry for the rest of his life.

See also Shūshin-koyō.

Tenbiki

Because of the **tenbiki** system it is rare for the Japanese corporate employee to receive his full salary each month. In accordance with the law, income tax is withheld at the source, as are payments for health and unemployment insurance and for social security. Under agreement between the company and the labor union, there is a checkoff for union dues.

Further deductions are arranged through agreement among the company, the employees, and the suppliers of various goods and services. These include installment payments for goods bought through the company, deposits for saving schemes, and premiums for group insurance. Then there are deductions based on company regulations, such as the rental fee for housing provided by the company.

Although these different types of **tenbiki** make the monthly pay envelope lighter, it is a convenient system about which employees have few complaints.

Tonosama-shōbai

The feudal lord (**tonosama**) did not engage in business (**shōbai**) as we know it today, but he had to deal with merchants in order to manage his domain. He lacked financial sense and was easily outwitted by merchants in money matters. Being in a high position, he was also accustomed to having people bow to him, even though they were actually his customers.

Today, when a big company with an illustrious tradition stagnates because it rests on its past glory and neglects to develop new products or to engage in vigorous marketing, people are apt to say, "Serves them right for doing **tonosama-shōbai.**" A similar term is **bushi no shōhō** (samurai's method of doing business). This was a scornful term used by merchants in reference to ex-samurai who tried to sell goods from a lofty posture and failed.

The opposite of these terms are **maedare-shōhō** and **maedare-seishin. Maedare** was the apron worn by an apprentice to merchant. A businessman who assumes a low posture and works diligently—just like the apprentices of old—is doing business in the **maedare** way **(shōhō)** or with the **maedare** spirit **(seishin).**

Tora

This is the ferocious tiger that abounds in China and Korea and in the old days often attacked human beings. The only place one finds tigers in Japan is the zoo. However, there are many Japanese paintings of tigers, stereotyped as lurking in a bamboo grove.

The bamboo leaf is known as **sasa** whose homonym is the ancient word for the rice wine **sake.** People may describe a drunkard as "a tiger from the **sasa**" or "you will become a tiger if you drink **sasa** and get drunk." Or, it might have been that a drunkard's bellow sounds like a tiger's roar or that the way a drunkard shakes his head is like a tiger.

At night, countless **tora** roam bar districts in big

cities. Some of them spend the night behind the bars not of a zoo but of a police station.

The tiger is known to take good care of its young (**ko**). Therefore, **tora-no-ko** is used to mean a precious belonging. Thus, "A burglar broke into her house last night and took her **tora-no-ko** diamond ring." The convenient reference book which students preparing for examination use is **tora-no-maki**. This comes from an ancient Chinese book on the art of war.

See also Aka-Chōchin.

Tozama

Tozama is a word symbolic of the way Japanese society is constituted. Directly translated, the word means "outside person" or "outsider."

In feudal days, it was customary for people to enter the service of a lord's family when very young and to serve for life, or for a son to follow in the footsteps of his father as a retainer to the same lord. Any person who entered the lord's service partway into his adult life was called a **tozama**.

Today, a person who is hired by a company not straight out of school but after spending some years in another organization is a **tomaza**. An **ama-kudari** person is also a **tozama**. In Japan's vertical society, a **tozama** is one who is not "purebred."

See also Ama-kudari, Teiki-sayō, Kogai.

Tsumaranai mono

A business acquaintance hands you a package and says, "This is a **tsumaranai mono** (worthless, insignificant thing), but please accept it as a gift." In such a case, it is better not to take the attitude, "If it's worthless I don't want it." It often turns out that when you open the package later, you will be surprised, because it contains an expensive item.

The word **soshina** written on **ochūgen** and **oseibo** gift packages is the literary word for the colloquial **tsumaranai mono.** Both words express the giver's humble attitude: "This may not be worth much to you, but I selected the best within my means."

When you sit down at the dinner table as an invited guest, you need not be surprised when the host says, "**Nani mo arimasen-ga** (we have nothing, but) please help yourself." As in the case of **soshina,** it means "We did our best to fix something that you might like, but if we are wrong, please forgive us." Go right ahead and partake heartily of the mountain of delicious food on the table.

Tsuru no hitokoe

One word (**hitokoe**) from the crane or stork (**tsuru**) often settles a matter decisively. Here, crane, of course, means a person of authority.

The crane is a bird that knows full well its weakness and is thus always on guard. It is a bird that seeks safety in acting together with its kind at all times. When a flock of cranes flies down on a bog and searches for food, one of its members always stands guard. The flock may be making a lot of clamor, but not because of imminent danger. But when the crane standing guard lets out a loud cry, it is a signal that danger is near and the entire flock takes off.

Tsuru no hitokoe, therefore, is the decisive voice coming from a man of authority. His voice overrules those of all others and is law. It is the **tsuru no hitokoe** that hands down the decision in an endless discussion. It is the word *ex cathedra*. It is the ruling handed down by the corporate president.

Uchi

Uchi means "inside," and the significance of this word in Japanese society is that it is used to demarcate what is "mine" and "ours" from what belongs to the "outside."

It is used in such ways as **uchi no kaisha** (our company), **uchi no hito** (my husband), **uchi no yatsu** (my wife), and **uchi no machi** (our town). All of these are often expressed simply as **uchi,** without adding the other words.

Thus, when **uchi** is used by itself, it can have different meanings. For instance, let us assume that three men who graduated from the same university but who now work in different departments of the same company are engaged in a conversation. When one of them says, "**Uchi no** business performance is better than that of other companies," he means "our company's." The second says, "**Uchi no** baseball team will win the national tournament," meaning "our alma mater's." "Unlike your boss, **uchi wa**—" means my boss. "**Uchi no wa** just entered kindergarten" means "my child."

Uchi very bluntly expresses the sense of identity. It refers to the place or group with which one has a sense of solidarity. The opposite is **soto** (outside) which at times is in an adversary relationship.

See also Gaijin.

Uchi-age

Uchi-age has two meanings. One is "shoot up" or "launch" things such as fireworks and artificial satellites. The other is "finish" or "close" a theatrical or entertainment performance. In the old days, when a theatrical engagement came to a close, people whooped it up with the lively beating of drums.

Today, when they complete a project, businessmen hold an **uchi-age** drinking party to celebrate the successful achievement of a target or their release from a hard task.

It is a sort of finale. This party also serves to consolidate the feeling of comradeship and solidarity among fellow workers. Of course, there are alcohol-lovers who organize an **uchi-age** party even for the completion of the smallest task.

At the party it is quite all right to pull out the stops (**hame wo hazusu**) within reason, but it is forbidden to foment trouble. The idea is to celebrate cheerfully, as if shooting off fireworks, and to replenish the spirit for a new task on the morrow. Of course, the **uchi-age** party is invariably followed by **hashigo-zake.**

See also Bureikō, Hame wo hazusu, Hashigo.

Umi-sen yama-sen

Umi is "sea," **sen** is "one thousand," and **yama** is "mountain." According to legend, a snake that has lived for a thousand years in the sea and another thousand years on the mountain will turn into a dragon and rise to heaven. From this, **umi-sen yama-sen** has come to mean a tough, wily man who has so much experience that he is rarely bested. However, it is not an expression of praise.

Anyone who addresses a bold and daring man toughened by many hard experiences, "You are **umi-sen yama-sen,** aren't you?" will surely receive a smashing right to the jaw. This is because you are saying he is a snake. Whether in the Occident or the Orient, the snake is considered to be a cunning and slimy creature, not at all lovable.

If you should be warned, "That fellow is an **umi-sen yama-sen no kuse-mono** (slippery character), so you better watch out," you should be prepared to have the most difficult time negotiating with him.

Undō-kai

"**Yōi don!**" (on your mark, get set, go!) and everybody starts running. The cheers of fellow workers and of your family members ring in your ears. You run with all your might. At the goal, not only the winner but all participants receive prizes. Superiors or subordinates, seniors or juniors, there is no such distinction. This is the **undō-kai** (field day).

Once a year, many schools, communities, and companies in Japan hold a field day. By participating in games and contests, the people reconfirm their feeling of belonging. This being the purpose, the performance is of secondary importance. Many of the events are ones in which anyone can take part regardless of sex or age—three-legged race, spoon race, shopping race, etc.

One of the characteristics of Japanese companies is the family-like relationship between the management and workers. Thus, **shain-ryokō, bōnenkai,** and **shin-nen-kai** are not the only functions held to strengthen the feeling of identity. Many companies also hold a **undō-kai.** The corporate president hands out prizes and gets to know the family members of the employees.

See also Bōnenkai, Shain-ryokō.

Uogokoro areba mizugokoro

This proverb is used most often in connection with male–female relationships. It means that if one side should display a favorable feeling toward the other, the other side would respond in like manner.

A rough translation of the expression would be "if the fish has a heart for the water, the water will have heart for the fish." It expresses like-mindedness or compatibility. In the business world it can be used to show a give-and-take relationship.

English sayings with a similar meaning are: Scratch my back and I'll scratch yours; do as you would have done to you; one hand washes the other.

Yabuhebi

The manager asks his people to make some suggestions on improving his department's operations. Back come a lot of complaints about what he is doing wrong and demands that he mend his ways about certain things. That wasn't what he expected. He has stirred up a hornet's nest, or in Japanese "**yabuhebi ni natta.**"

A staff member may make a suggestion which the manager says is excellent, and to the proposer's surprise he is assigned to implement the idea, which requires a lot of hard extra work. Again, **yabuhebi.**

The word **yabuhebi** translates literally as "snake in the bush," and it means "stirring up the snake lying peacefully in the bush." So, if you want to say, "Let a sleeping dog lie" or "Don't stir up a hornet's nest," the expression to use in Japanese is: **Sore wa yabuhebi ni narimasu yo.**

Yakudoshi

One may assume that without a scientific and practical mind, the Japanese would not have been able to reach their present high level of technical and industrial development. As a corollary one might think that such a people would have little use for superstitious beliefs. But no.

Many things in Japanese society are governed by superstitious beliefs. **Yakudoshi** is just one of them. This is the belief that men and women have a predetermined unlucky age when all sorts of misfortune are likely to visit them. During a person's unlucky age, he/she might become extraordinarily cautious and refrain from doing things that ordinarily would be routine.

A man's **yakudoshi** is forty-two, and a woman's

thirty-three. Minor unlucky ages in the man's case are twenty-five and sixty. A woman has only one minor unlucky age: nineteen.

Yakutoku

This word describes an extra benefit or gain in addition to the regular salary, which one enjoys because of the post he holds. When the man who is in charge of choosing the supplies the company buys is entertained or receives **ochūgen** and **oseibo** gifts, it is a case of **yakutoku.**

If a man in such a post gets influenced by the **yakutoku** and makes decisions in favor of the supplier. If he should ask for additional considerations, he will not only be regarded with contempt but will also face the danger of his actions coming to light. A government official caught in such an act would be dismissed for accepting bribery, while in a business firm the man's promotion would be adversely affected.

Cases of a person directly requesting **yakutoku** are few. Most of the time, it is through **ishindenshin** (communication of thought without the medium of words). Sometimes, a man who receives an expensive gift would fly into a rage, "Don't insult me!" He is outraged because he thinks the other party regards him as a man with a bad heart. Gifts are for smoothing human relations, so care must be taken not to exceed the bounds. Otherwise a gift will have an adverse effect.

See also Gyōsha, Ishin-denshin, Shayō-zoku.

Yanagi no shita

The full expression is **yanagi no shita no nihikime no dojō** (the second loach under the willow tree). This saying is often used by businessmen to mean that since the first project was a success, a similar success is also anticipated in the second project.

Actually, the original proverb from which this saying stemmed has quite a different context. The original is **yanagi no shita ni itsumo dojō wa inai** (You won't always find a loach under the willow tree). This means that just because a loach (**dojō**) was caught once in the pond under (**shita**) the willow tree (**yanagi**), it does not follow that a second one would be caught in the same place. In effect, "Good luck does not always repeat itself."

The reverse of this often happens in business: One hit is followed by another. Thus, businessmen coined the new expression—hopefully.

Incidentally, the loach is a small fish about 10 centimeters long with slimy scales. It is used as the ingredient for soup and chowder.

See also Niban-senji.

Yoko-meshi

Yoko is lateral or horizontal and **meshi** is meal (lunch or dinner), but if the word is rendered in English as "horizontal meal" it makes no sense. Here, **yoko** is a reference to English or European languages, which are written on a horizontal line as opposed to the vertical writing of the Japanese. Thus **yoko-meshi** becomes a business lunch or dinner with visitors from overseas.

Although the Japanese start learning English at the age of twelve in junior high school and continue through senior high school and part of university, they don't seem to make much progress. Thus, eating a meal while conversing in English requires concentration on language. So they say, "When I have **yoko-meshi** I don't feel as if I had a meal." Perhaps the readers of this book who are not fluent in Japanese may feel that a **tate-meshi** (vertical meal) is similarly something of an ordeal.

Yoroshiku

When parting after a negotiation or a meeting, Japanese businessmen more often than not say "goodbye" with a **yoroshiku** instead of a **sayonara**. When people are introduced or meet for the first time, they also say **yoroshiku** to each other. When a person asks another to convey his best wishes to someone else, he says, "Please say **yoroshiku** to Mr. X."

This versatile word conveys a variety of meanings. In the first case above, it may be "I'm depending on you," "I hope you will take proper action," "Please give it your consideration," "I hope you will give us a favorable reply," etc. Usually the matter in question is not mentioned in concrete terms.

In the second case, it is used in the same way as "How do you do?" or "Pleased to meet you," and carries the nuance of "I hope you will be favorably disposed toward me." In the third case, **yoroshiku** means "Give my best regards to" or "Remember me to Mr. X".

Yūkyū-kyūka

This is the term for paid leave. Salaried workers in Japan are given twenty or so paid holidays per year in addition to Sundays, twelve national holidays and, if their company has adopted the five-day week, Saturdays.

The number of paid holidays depends on the length of service. Generally, it starts with seven days for the first year and increases by two days each year up to a maximum of twenty.

The older generation, particularly white-collar businessmen, often do not take all the **yūkyū-kyūka** to which they are entitled, because, many say, they are too busy. The younger generation takes paid vacations for granted, and their life-style is influencing the older corporate employees.

It has now become customary for most salaried workers to take a weeklong vacation in summer, if they can adjust their work arrangements to make it possible.

See also Kaki-kyūka.

Zangyō

Zangyō (remain behind to work) is the Japanese word for overtime. Working overtime is very common in Japanese companies, so much so that workers count upon receiving a certain amount of overtime pay (**zangyō teate**) regularly every month. This is particularly so among factory workers.

Among younger workers, an increasing number prefer more free time than overtime pay, which is about twenty percent more than regular wages.

Although overtime compensation is not paid to

people in managerial positions, generally from section chief level up, they remain behind after working hours more than anybody else—perhaps from a sense of responsibility or loyalty to the company, or desire to be noticed for promotion, or just for love of work.

See also Teate.

Zensho shimasu

Zensho shimasu is an expression with an affirmative, positive tone: "I shall do my best to respond to your wishes" or "I shall deal with it accordingly" or "I'll attend to it in a suitable manner" or "I'll fix it up for you." It is a widely used expression in business and life in general.

If you point out to a customer that he hasn't been paying his bills regularly, he will say "**Zensho shimasu.**" If you complain that the manufacturer has been sending you substandard goods, he will say "**Zensho shimasu.**"

It should be noted that the expression does not commit the speaker to a concrete course of action. It's a general "I'll do my best." Sometimes it happens that you feel relieved by the **zensho shimasu,** but the implied action is not taken. The explanation, in such cases, will invariably be "Oh, I tried my best, but—."

See also Kangaete okimasu.

Index

abacus (*soroban*), 146–47
Achilles' heel, bugaboo (*kimon*), 79–80; (*naki dokoro*), 99
active, nimble (*koshi ga karui*), 82
address, terms of: honorific, respectful (*sensei*), 130–31; Mr., Ms. (*-san*), 125–26
advancement of schedule (*maedaoshi*), 88–89
advantage, benefit (*miso*), 92; added (*kamo-negi*), 68; 138; turn facts to one's own (*gaden-insui*), 94
see also perquisites
Aesop's Fables, 62
aging, 73–74, 118
alcohol, 13–14, 20–21, 30, 31, 45, 164
see also drinking; sake
allowances, increments, 153 (*teate*), 157
overtime (*zangyō teate*), 171
retirement, 79, 158
see also salary
alumni (*dōsōsei*), 26–27
connections among (*gaku-batsu*), 11; and between older (*senpai*) and younger grad (*kōhai*), 129–30

amateur performance
see backup cassette; talent, hidden
ambiguity, equivocation (*tamamushi-iro*), 151–52
aplomb, poise (*hidari-uchiwa*), 46
apple polisher, sycophant, toady (*gomasuri*), 35–36; (*koshiginchaku*), 60–61
see also flattery
appointment (*apointo*), 6
apprentice, disciple (*kogai*), 80–81
armchair, executive (*hijikake-isu*), 46–47
assertive, pushy (*karewa aku ga tsuyoi*), 4

back-scratcher (*mago-no-te*), 75
see also reciprocity
backer, patron (*dorubako; kane-zuru*), 25; form a group of (*mikoshi wo katsugu*), 91; serve as (*kata wo ireru*), 73
backup cassette (*kara-oke*), 72
bailiwick, turf (*nawabari*), 100–101
bargaining, 12, 51, 54–55 (*suri-awase*), 148–49 (*tataku*), 155; collective, 143

"batching it" (*-chon*), 17–18, 153
behind-scenes operator, manipulator (*newaza-shi*), 103–4
bellwether, kingpin (*daikoku-bashira*), 21
belonging, sense of: mine, ours (*uchi*), 163–64; theirs (*soto*), 164
see also camaraderie; in-house; outsider
big shot (*ōmono*), 117
big talk, blowhard (*hora wo yū; hora wo fuku*), 16, 110 (*oburoshiki*), 109–10
see also self-advertisement
bigmouth (*kōzetsu no to*), 140–41
bonus (*bōnasu*), 12–13, 55; for stockholders, 146
born-and-bred, purebred (*haenuki*), 38–39
boss, 8, 20, 45, 55, 60, 78, 80, 81, 108, 133
disdainful treatment by (*ago de ashirau*), 1
going over head of (*jikiso*), 105
overbearing (*ago de tsukau*), 1
bribe (*sode-no-shita*): acceptance of (*sode-no-shita wo tsukau*), 144; offer of (*sode-no-shita wo morau*), 144
Buddhism, 15, 33, 47–48; priest of (*bōzu*), 15, 110
bureaucracy, civil service, 11, 26, 37, 50, 73, 154
business cards, calling cards (*meishi*), 30, 91, 150
business lunch, 82; with foreigners (*yoko-meshi*), 169–70
business meeting, 86, 111
business trip (*shutchō*), 128
businessman, 21, 30, 41–42, 55, 65, 69, 81, 91, 109, 125, 145, 170
common touch of (*maedare shōhō*), 160
family life of, 17–18, 65, 89–90, 128, 153
foreign, 2, 6, 39, 64, 90, 102, 152

goldbricking, loafing (*abura wo uru*), 1
high-handed methods of (*tono-sama-shubai; bushi no shōhō*), 159–60
Japanese, 6, 13, 29–30, 55, 59, 65, 69, 89–90, 91, 145, 153
busy season (*kaki-ire-doki*), 64–65
buzzard, wily old (*umi-sen yama-sen*), 164–65

cafeteria or commissary, company (*shain-shokudō*), 133
calculator, 146
camaraderie, group spirit, 66, 69–70, 119, 132, 137, 165–66
can of worms, hornet's nest (*yabu-hebi*), 166–67
cantankerous (*heso-magari; tsumuji-magari*), 45
capital, 25
Chamber of Commerce, Japan, 146
character, temperament (*hada*), 37–38
cheer, hurrah, viva (*banzai*), 10, 146
chestnuts, pulling out of fire (*kachū-ne-kuri wo hirou*), 62; saving another's butt (*shiri-nugui*), 140
chief of staff, right-hand man (*futokoro-gatana*), 27, 117
China, 28, 57, 63, 98, 104, 160
chivalry, romanticism (*naniwa bushi*), 99–100
circumspection (*saji-kagen wo suru*), 125
civil service
see bureaucracy; government
coffee breaks, 1 (*ocha wa nomu*), 111–12
cohort, contemporaries (*dōki*), 23, 137
communication: indirect (*hara-gei*), 42; nonverbal, telepathic (*ishin-denshin*), 56, 168; social, 69; word-of-mouth, grapevine (*kuchi-komi*), 141

company housing (sha-taku), 132
compatibility (hada ni au), 38 (ki ni
    iru), 78
complacency (nuruma-yu), 108–109
computer, 146
conference (kaigi), 64
Confucius, 57
connections, personal (jin-myaku),
    59, 95; through shared experi-
    ence (onaji kama no meshi), 118–
    19
contacts, business: influential (kao
    ga kiku), 71; keeping up (kao wo
    tsunagu), 71; personal, many
    (kao ga hiroi), 71
contracts, 77, 97, 106
copy, rip-off, sequel (niban-senji),
    104; hopeful (yanagi no shita),
    104, 169
coquette (kamatoto; burikko), 67; ag-
    ing (kamakujira), 67
corresponding period of previous
    year (dōki), 23
courteous (hada-zawari ga yawara-
    kai), 38
courtesy calls (aisatsu-mawari), 2–3,
    29
see also contacts, keeping up
crucial confrontation (Sekigahara;
    Tennōzan), 128–29; labor-
    management (shuntō), 143
curiosity-seeker, rubberneck (yaji-
    uma), 9
cutting corners (te wo nuku), 156

debt: forgiveness of (chara ni suru),
    16; up to neck in (kubi ga mawa-
    sarai), 84
deception, eyewash (chara), 16
decision-making: conferring prior
    to (jingi wo kiru), 57–58; by
    consensus (kaigi), 64, 102; en-
    listing prior assent in (nema-
    washi), 58, 102, 123, 149 (suri-
    awase), 148–49; leaving to oth-
    ers (geta wo azukeru), 31–32

decoy, stalking horse (ate-uma), 8
deliberations: endless, fruitless
    (odawara-hyōjō), 112, 163; moot
    (mizu-kake-ron), 94
deus ex machina (kamikaze), 66
disagreeable, displeasing (ki ni ku-
    wanai), 78
discount, price, 155 (benkyō), 12
    (sābisu), 124
disheveled, frazzled (ōwarawa), 121
diversification (atarashī shōbai ni te
    wo tsukeru), 156
documents, forms: memorandum,
    122; notification (todoke), 101–
    102; request (negai), 101–102;
    routing list (ringi-sho), 122–23
dormitory, company, 119 (shain-
    ryō), 132; for bachelors
    (tanshin-ryō), 132
double-checking, checking back
    (dame-oshi), 22; making sure
    (kugi wo sasu), 85–86
doyen (ōgosho), 112
draft proposal (tataki-dai), 155
drinking, 2, 13–14, 20–21, 45, 52, 63,
    101, 164; heavy drinker (hidari-
    kiki; satō), 31 (tora), 160–61;
    nondrinker (geko), 30–31
see also alcohol; sake
drinking establishments, 20–21, 70,
    101, 138, 149
bar, pub (aka-chōchin), 2, 3, 45, 52,
    72, 124, 135, 160 (nawa-noren), 3
cabaret, 70
nightclub, 82, 93, 135
dumbstruck (shita wo maku), 141
duty: beyond call of, supereroga-
    tion (katte-deru), 74; demean-
    ing (miya-zukae), 93; sense of
    (giri-gatai hito), 33

easing out of office (mawata de kubi
    wo shimeru), 85
education, 13, 18, 28–29, 103
eloquent (kuchi hatchō), 141
empty title (hashigo wo hazu-sareru),

44 (*madogiwa-zoku*), 87–88, 114,
152
envy (*oka-yaki*), 116; expressions of,
4, 14, 60, 139, 155
etiquette, terms of, 126
appreciation (*gokurō-sama*), 35
(*kekkō desu*), 76–77
emphasis (*domō*), 24–25
excuse me (*chotto*), 20 (*shitsurei
shimasu*), 141–42
got a minute? (*ohima desuka?*), 114
gratitude (*otsukare-sama*), 35
offering meal (*nani mo arimasen-
ga*), 162
one moment, please (*chotto
matte*), 20
sorry (*sumimasen*), 24, 147
thank you (*arigatō*), 24
see also goodbye; greetings; harmony, social; responses
exhaustion, overwork (*ago wo dasu*),
2 (*gogatsu-byō*)
expense account, 122; for entertainment (*kosai-hi*), 81–82, 135,
150; plutocrats on (*shayō-zoku*),
134

face: causing loss of (*kao wo tsubusu*), 71; loss of, 45; saving another's (*kao wo tateru*), 71
fair play, 138
fall for a swindle (*ippai kū*), 52 (*ejiki
ni sareta*), 68
see also snow job
family ties (*kei-batsu*), 11; "like family" (*giri no naka*), 33
see also obligation
female employees, 24, 76, 127, 134
(*shokuba no hana*), 41 (*OL*),
116–17
feudal Japan, 5, 26, 27, 37, 46, 57,
62, 67, 73, 79, 81, 92, 96, 100,
112, 118, 119, 123, 159, 161
see also samurai, shogun
filling in time, waiting (*ma wo motasu*), 86–87

final say (*tsuru no hitokoe*), 162–63
financial distress (*hi-no-kuruma*), 48
flattery, 8, 17, 35–36
flunky (cha-bōzu), 15–16, 60 (*kaban-
mochi*), 60–61
following the crowd (*chōchin wo
tsukeru*), 17
foreigners, 20, 23, 52–53, 141 (*gaijin*), 28, 115; Chinese (*tōjin*), 28
see also West, Westerners
forerunner (*yobi-mizu*), 94
forked tongue (*nimai-jita*), 140
formality, 56 (*jingi wo kiru*), 57–58
four-flusher, phony (*charan-poran*),
16
franchising (*noren-wake*), 107
free ride (*oyakata hinomaru*), 121–22

gambling, 63, 74
games: athletic meet, 146 (*undō-kai*),
165–66; bridge, 19; cards (*hana-
garuta*), 18; buying in (*katte-
deru*), 74; chess (*shōgi*), 18; go,
85, 115; mah jongg, 18, 114
getting down to business (*koshi wo
sueru*), 83
gift-giving, 161–62; "it's nothing
much" (*tsumaranai mono; soshina*), 161–62; midsummer
(*ochūgen*), 32, 64, 71, 144, 154,
168; year-end (*oseibo*), 32, 64,
71, 144, 154, 168
glimmer of hope (*myaku ga aru*), 95–
96
glory, laurels (*hana*), 40–41; seeking
of, 107–8
go-getter, live wire (*kiremono*), 49;
quality of (*kaishō; kaigai-shii*),
63
gobbledygook (*tamamushi-iro*), 150–
51
godsend
see luck; windfall
goldmine, profit center (*dorubako*),
25
good-for-nothing (*kaishō-nashi*), 63

goodbye (*sayonara*), 140 (*shitsurei shimasu*), 141–42 (*yoroshiku*), 170
government, Japanese, 37, 48, 121–22
  budget, 88
  Diet, 151
  employees of, 73–74, 93, 129, 142, 144
  legislators, 120, 130, 153
  officials, 100
  retirees from (*ama-kudari*), 4–5, 39, 47, 161
gratis, premium (*sabisu*), 124
gray area (*hai-iro*), 151
great leader (*ōmono; daijinbitsu*), 117
greed, 120
greetings: be right with you (*tadaima*), 149–50; hi—I'm back (*tadaima*), 149; how do you do (*yoroshiku*), 170; how's it going? (*dochira-e?*), 22–23; keeping busy? (*oisogashii desuka?*), 113–14; may I help you? (*irasshai mase? rasshai*), 52–53; welcome back (*okaeri-nasai*), 149
gumption, grit (konjō), 80, 125

hand-to-mouth, shoestring operation (*jitensha-sōgyō*), 48
hanger-on (*koshi-ginchaku*), 60–61
harmony, social, 32, 56, 69, 82, 100, 168
haughty (*koshi ga takai*), 82; in business practice (*tonosama shubai; bushi no shōhō*), 159–60
have a hand in (*katabō wo katsugu*), 72–73
"having it made"
  see worry-free state
head-hunting, personnel (*hikinuki*), 47, 142 (*chūto-saiyo*), 158, 161
heart (*ki*), 78–79
  eat one's out (*naki-neiri*), 99
  loss of (*ki wo nuku*), 78

no enthusiasm for (*ki ga hairanu*), 78 (*oyobi-goshi*), 83
  in right place (*ki wa kokoro*), 78
  troubled (*ki wo momu*), 78
heart-to-heart talk, 2 (*hara wo watte hanasu*), 43
henpeck (*teishu wo shiri ni shiku*), 140
hiring, 4, 5–6, 158, 161
  see also head-hunting; recruitment
hogging, to allocate to oneself (*otemori*), 120
holidays, 90, 155
  Christmas, 91
  company anniversary (*sōritsu-kinenbi*), 145–46
  feast days, 40
  flower festivals, 9
  leave (*kyūka*), 128; menstrual (*seiri-kyūka*), 127–28; paid (*yūkyū-kyūka*), 171
  New Year, 2, 29, 36, 71, 91, 121
  summer vacation (*kaki-kyūka*), 65, 171
  year-end, 2
  see also gift-giving; parties
homebody, non-careerist (*mai-hōmu shugisha*), 89–90
human relations
  see harmony, social
humble (*koshi ga hikui*), 82
humiliation, 93

identity or image, corporate, 127, 137, 166
  anthem (*shaka*), 19, 133–34
  badge, insignia, 127, 134
  code of conduct (*shafu*), 131–32
  company anniversary (*sōritsu-kinenbi*), 145–46
  history, 146
  motto, watchword (*shaze*), 19, 136
  slogan (*shakun*), 136
imprimatur, authentication (*osumitsuki*), 119–20
in-group (*batsu*), 10–11, 33

in-house, intramural (*sha-nai*), 134–
35
see also belonging
informality (*bureikō*), 3, 14–15, 20,
40, 133
ingrate (*on-shirazu; on wo ada de
kaesu*), 118
inhibitions, shedding of (*hame wo
hazusu*), 40, 133, 164
inopportune, untoward (*ma ga
warui*), 87
instinctive dislike (*mushi ga
sukanai*), 44
intention, objective (*honne*), 45, 51,
(*te no uchi*), 155
interest, spark of (*iroke*), 53–54
inventory: book (*chōbo-tana-
oroshi*), 152; loss from (*tana-
oroshi-zon*), 152; taking of
(*tana-oroshi*), 152
invitation to retire (*kata-tataki*), 71–
72
involvement, getting involved
(*koshi wa ageru*), 82–83

jerk, nitwit (*ma-nuke*), 87
jumping the gun (*nukegake*), 107–8

Kabuki theater, 41, 93, 113
karma, relatedness (*go-en*), 33–34,
115
keystone, linchpin (*yatai-bone*), 21
kingmaker, power broker (*kuromaku*), 86

Labor Standards Law, 127–28
labor unions, 13, 54, 129, 143, 159;
and checkoff system, 159; Sohyo, Domei, 143
lantern, Japanese (*chōchin*), 3, 17
largess (*on*), 118
layoffs, 70
lifetime employment system
(*shūshin-koyō*), 56, 79, 88, 136,
143, 158
living off father (*sune-kajiri*), 147–48

lonely, unaided struggle (*hitori-
zumō wo totte-iro*), 49–50
loss leader (*mizuhiki torihiki*), 94
low-status jobs (*hiya-meshi-kui*), 50–
51
luck (*ma*), 86–87; stroke of (*tanabota-
shiki*), 151–52
see also misfortune; unlucky age;
windfall

management, 129, 131–32; Japanese
style of, 64
managers, top, 11, 47, 49, 60, 122,
166–67
board of directors, 14, 136, 152
brought in from outside (*ama-
kudari*), 4–5, 39, 47, 122
division chief (*buchō*), 14, 126
section chief (*kachō*), 14, 61–62,
103
subsection chief (*kakarichō*), 14,
103
top aide (*futokoro-gatana*), 27, 49
women as, 117
see also president, corporate
marketing, 104; emphasis on (*niban-
te shōhō*), 104
markup in price (*geta wo haku*), 32
marriage, 32; in-house (*sha-nai kekkon*), 133
maverick, solo operator (*nukegake*),
107–8
"May sickness," letdown (*gogatsu-
byō*), 34–35
Meiji Restoration, 117
Mencius, 57
Ministry of International Trade and
Industry, 62
misfortunes, one after another
(*naki-tsura ni hachi*), 99
missing the boat, tardiness (*ato-no-
matsuri*), 9
mistake, goof, oversight (*chonbo*),
18–19 (*miso wo tsukeru; miso ga
tsuku*), 92; slip-up (*te-ochi*), 156
misunderstanding, 39, 69

money collector (*tsuke-uma*), 8
money-grubbing (*gyōsha*), 37
Mongols, 67
mores, family (*ka-fū*), 131-32

negotiation: business, 51, 68, 77, 80,
    81, 89, 125, 145, 156, 165; indi-
    rect (*hara-gei*), 42; labor, 129,
    143; plea for concessions in
    (*soko wo nantoka*), 145; of sale
    (*te wo utsu*), 156
nightclub
    see drinking establishments
night owl, pub-crawler (*gozen-
    sama*), 52
nitpicking (*tana-oroshi*), 152

obdurate (*te ni amaru*), 156
obligation, social (*giri*), 32-33, 97,
    100, 118; *noblesse oblige*, 45; to
    parents (*oya no on*), 118; repay-
    ment of (*giri wo hatasu*), 32-33
    (*on-gaeshi*), 118
    see also duty
observer, disinterested (*okame-
    hachimoku*), 115-16
outsider (*tozama*), 39, 81, 161
    see also foreigner
overcautious (*ishibashi wo tataku*),
    55-56
    see also double-checking
overnight success (*nari-agari; nari-
    kin*), 154-55
overtime (*zangyō*), 171-72

panic (*koshi ga nukeru*), 83
parties, 113, 129; New Year, for
    business associates (*gashi-
    kōkan*), 29-30
parties, company of office, 40, 66,
    86, 133
    anniversary (*sōritsu kinenbi*), 145-
    46
    celebrating end of task (*uchi-age*),
    164
    changeover (*kansūgei-kai*), 70

New Year (*shin-nen-kai*), 14, 29-
    30, 166
    outing (*shain-ryokō*), 15, 132-33,
    135, 166
    send-off (*sōbetsu-kai*), 70
    welcoming (*kangei-kai*), 69-70
    year-end (*bōnen-kai*), 13, 15, 166
payroll deductions (*tenbiki*), 159
pension, 74
pep talk, 81 (*chōrei*), 19
perquisites, side benefits (*yaku-
    toku*), 168
personnel moves: amicable depar-
    ture (*enman taisha*), 57; annual
    (*jinji-idō*), 58-59; assignment,
    23, 69, 126-27, 137, 139; away
    from family (*tanshin-funin*), 17-
    18, 128, 153; between compan-
    ies, 4-5; demotion (*sasen*), 126-
    27; dismissal, 26, 79 (*kubi ga
    tobu*), 84; notification of (*jirei*),
    59-60; on loan (*shukkō-shain*),
    142; promotion, 5, 23, 44-45,
    47, 50, 54, 58, 59, 74, 103, 120;
    to provinces (*dosa mawari*), 26
    (*sasen; tobasu*), 126-27; and reas-
    signment, 120, 135; staff cuts
    (*kubi-kiri*), 84
    see also layoffs; recruitment; resig-
    nation; retirement
pettishness (*heso wo nageru; tsumuji
    wo mageru*), 45
piece of cake, snap (*asameshi-mae;
    ocha-no-ko*), 7-8, 111
piecework, home (*naishoku*), 96-97
pigeon, pushover, sucker (*kamo;
    magamo*), 68
political parties, 149, 153; factions of
    (*ha-batsu*), 11
popularity, businesses dependent
    on (*mizu-shōbai*), 93
power, rule (*tenka*), 5, 129
practice (*keiko*), 76-77
preliminary measures (*te wo utsu*),
    156
premonition (*mushi ga shiraseru*),
    43-44

president, corporate, 2, 14, 47, 55, 63, 80, 105, 123, 136, 166 (*sha-chō*), 126; authoritative word of (*tsuru no hitokoe*), 162–63; retirement of (*hana-michi wo kazaru*), 41

prettify, whitewash (*ocha wo nigosu*), 111

pride and joy (*iki-gai*), 63

prig (*heso-magari*), 45–46

principles, posture (*tatemae*), 51

problem-solving, 42, 137; by consensus (*kaigi*), 64

profit-sharing, 13

promotion
see personnel moves

promotion ladder (*hashigo*), 44–45, 86, 88, 101, 129

puffery (*chōchin-kiji*), 17

pulse-taking (*dashin suru; myaku wo miru*), 96

pump-priming (*mae-daoshi*), 88

quixotic
see chivalry

racing one's motor (*kara-mawari*), 121

rack one's brain (*kubi wo hineru*), 84

recession, 70, 79, 82, 150

reciprocity, one hand washes the other (*uogokoro areba mizugokoro*), 166

recruitment, 5–6, 47, 58, 69, 136, 144, 156; annual (*teiki-saiyo*), 157–58; and recruits (*shin-nyū-shain*), 136–37; of specialists (*chūto-saiyo*), 158
see also head-hunting; hiring; schools

regional ties (*chihō-batsu*), 11

reputation (*noren*), 107–8, 137; blot on (*miso wo tsukeru; miso ga tsuku*), 92; staking one's, 106 (*kubi wo kakete*), 84
see also face; "stock"

resignation, 34; letter of (*jihyō*), 56–57; offer of (*shintai-ugaki*), 137–38; voluntary (*kibō-taishoku*), 79, 144

response to proposal, query: evasive (*cha ni suru*), 110; facetious (*cha wo yū*), 111; fine, thanks (*okagesamade*), 114–15; forget it, no way (*kangaete okimasu*), 68–69, 89; I'll try my best (*zensho shimasu; maemukini zensho shimasi*), 89, 172; just maybe (*maemukini kangaete okimasu*), 69; killing with silence (*nigiri tsubushi*), 105; no (*te*), 39 (*kangaete okimasu*), 68–69; noncommittal (*tamamushi-iro*), 150–51; shelving it (*tana-age*), 105; so-so (*mā-mā*), 90–91 (*mā-mā desu*), 114; yes (*hai*), 49

restaurants, 53, 93, 124, 133, 149

retirement, 41, 60, 73–74, 79, 88 (*teinen*), 158; age of, 79, 142, 152, 158; power in (*insei*), 112–13
see also president, corporate

risk-taking (*koketsu-ni-irazumba: koji wo ezu*), 62–63 (*kubi wo kakete*), 84; with career (*datsu-sara*), 108

rough edges, smoothing of (*suri-awase*), 148–49

rub the wrong way (*hada ni awanai*), 38

rubber stamp (*sanmon-ban*), 42

runaround (tarai-mawashi), 153–54
see also bureaucracy

sacrificial lamb (*shiraha-no-ya*), 139

sake, 3, 31, 45, 52, 69, 82, 160
see also alcohol

salary, 12, 54–55, 79, 143, 157, 159, 168, 171; raises, 138, 143; risk-taking, 108; service system, length of (*nenkō-joretsu*), 102–3, 150, 171
see also allowances

salt (*shio*), 138

samurai, 15, 46, 57, 96, 118, 121, 123, 138, 160

schemer (*hara-guroi*), 43

schools, 26–27, 47, 59, 80, 129, 130, 136, 148, 157, 165; for abacus operation, 146; background (*gakureki*), 28–29; exams, 161; recruitment from (*aota-gai; aota-gari*), 5–6, 136

scuttlebutt, speculation (*gebahyō*), (*shimbun jirei*), 30

seal, personal (*hanko*), 41–42, 123

seating order, pecking order (*sekiji*), 129

second chance, plea for (*naki wo ireru*), 99

secretaries, 14, 22, 133; executive (*kaban-mochi*), 60–61

secrets, company (*sha-gai-hai*), 135

section structure, corporate (*kasei*), 61–62

self-advertisement (*kao wo uru*), 71, (*temae-miso*), 92

self-made (*tataki-age*), 154–55

send-off (*goshūgi*), 36; party for (*sobetsu-kai*), 70

seniority system, 58, 88; and time in grade (*sekiji*), 129

service
see treatment

service industry, 74–75; aiming to please in (*kayui-tokoro ni te ga todoku*), 75; and failing (*kakka-sōyō*), 75

shinto, 91

shogun, 4, 15, 30, 96, 112, 116, 119

slack season (*kanko-doi ga naku*), 70 (*nippachi*), 105–106

slow starter (*keikōtō*), 48 (*shiri ga omoi*), 139–40
see also sluggish

sluggish (*kinori usu*), 78–79 (*koshi ga omoi*), 82

smooth-talking (*shitasaki-sanzun*), 139

snow job (*kemu ni maku*), 77 (*kuchi-guruma ni noseru*), 140

sour grapes (*suppai budō*), 62

speak one's mind (*hara wo miseru*), 43

spinelessness (*shiri no ana ga chii-sai*), 140

sports, 75–76; fencing (*kendō*), 75; *jūdō*, 49, 75, 103; "no contest" (*sumō ni naranai*), 49; *sumō*, 49, 73, 83, 138

status, 150
see also seating order

"stock," personal prestige: rising (*kabu ga ageru*), 61; dropping, falling (*kabu ga sageru*), 61

stock market, 17, 36, 79; Kabutocho (financial district), 30

stool pigeon (*okappiki*), 116

stores, 12, 31, 53, 124, 150; busy season of (*kaki-ire-doki*), 64–65; department, 53, 64, 127; reputation of (*noren*), 106–107; supermarkets, 12, 127

strategic pause (*ma wo ireru*), 87

straw matting (*tatami*), 133

stress, 34–35, 44

strikes, 13

stupidity, 19, 131

stymied (*o-te-age*), 156

suicide, 34, 65–66 (*hara-kiri*), 27, 43 (*seppuku*), 43

suspense, kept in (*ki wo momaseru*), 78

swallow the pill (*hara wo kukuru*), 43

sweetening an offer (*iro wo tsukeru*), 54–55

talent: acquisition, development of (*keiko-goto; o-keiko; ressun*), 76; expert (*ohako*), 113; hidden (*kakushi-gei*), 65–66, 76

tantrum (*kan no mushi*), 44

taxes, 30; income, 159

tea (*cha*), 15, 104, 110–12; ceremony, 76

thumbing nose (*shiri wo makeru*), 140

throw in towel (*saji wo nageru*), 124–25
touching base (*jingi wo kiru*), 57–58
 see also courtesy calls
training, 137
treatment, service (*taigu*), 150
two-income household (*tomo bataraki; tomo-kasegi*), 96

underachiever, do-nothing (*nazaku tobazu*), 98
underworld, 26, 57–58, 71, 100 (*yakuza*), 100
unemployment, 122–23; insurance, 159; voluntary (*rōnin*), 96, 122–23
uniforms, company (*seifuku*), 127, 134
universities, 29, 47, 60, 103, 136, 157, 170; entrance examinations to, 34, 123
unknown quantity, nonentity (*hiruandon*), 48–49
unlucky age (*yakudoshi*), 167–68
unmarried employees (*dokushin-kizuku*), 24, 116–17, 147–48

valuables (*tora-no-ko*), 161
volunteering (*katte-deru*), 74

Waterloo, 128
way-station, career stopping place (*koshikake*), 83–84
wear out one's welcome (*mikoshi wo suete hanashi-komu*), 92
West, Westerners, 19, 22, 36, 56, 62, 115, 129, 131, 133 (*i-jin; ketō*), 28
wet blanket (*mizu wo sasu*), 94
white-collar workers, 127, 142, 171
 see also secretaries
wimp (*kare wa aku no nuketa*), 4 (*konjo ga nai*), 81 (*koshi-kudake*), 83
windfall, godsend (*kamikaze ga fuku*), 67 (*tanabota*), 151–52
wipe slate clean (*mizu ni nagasu*), 94; (*nakatta-koto ni suru*), 97–98
work: free-lance, part-time, temporary (*arubaito*), 6–7, 96; home piecework (*naishoku*), 96–97
workaholic, 90 (*mōretsu shain*), 95
World War II, 13, 28, 68, 95
worry-free state (*hidari-uchiwa*), 46, 158; at work (*ōbune ni noru*), 109
wrong side of bed, got up on (*mushi no idokoro ga warui*), 44